shades of winter

KNITTING WITH
natural wool

INTERWEAVE.
interweave.com

INGALILL JOHANSSON // EWA K. ANDINSSON

TRANSLATOR // Carol Huebscher Rhoades
EDITOR // Erica Smith
TECHNICAL EDITOR // Therese Chynoweth
ART DIRECTOR // Liz Quan
DESIGNER // Julia Boyles
ILLUSTRATOR // Therese Chynoweth
PHOTOGRAPHER // Ewa K. Andinsson
PRODUCTION DESIGNER // Katherine Jackson

Interweave Press LLC
201 East Fourth Street
Loveland, CO 80537-5655 USA
Interweave.com

Printed in China by C&C Offset

Library of Congress
Cataloging-in-Publication Data
Johansson, Ingalill, 1955–
[Stickat i ekologisk ull. English]
Shades of winter / Ingalill Johansson and
Ewa K. Andinsson ; translation by Carol
Huebscher Rhoades.
pages cm
ISBN 978-1-59668-786-8 (pbk.)
1. Knitting--Patterns. I. Andinsson, Ewa K.,
1965– II. Title.
TT825.J6313 2012
746.43'2--dc23
2012018527

10 9 8 7 6 5 4 3 2 1

Acknowledgments

A personal thank you to my children, Oskar and Ebba, who have put up with yarn all over the house and a constantly working mother. Thanks also to my parents, Evy and Olle Johansson, for being there for me. Ewa K. Andinsson for her fantastic photos, support, and friendship. Without you, this book would not have happened.

Barbro Hagelin, Barbro Schönbeck, Elisabeth Röhr, Lena Fallquist, and Rigmor Åhren, who knit many of the book's garments. Inger Kjellberg for proofreading.

We have had incredible support from many companies and individuals. Thank you to the Icehotel at Jukkasjärvi for the fairy-tale environment and pleasant meetings and to Johanna Tiensuu-Stålnacke for professional project leadership during our time there.

SAS for kind treatment on our trip to Kiruna. Hovås Kallbadhus for arranging such a pretty setting. Avenue Models and the book's two brilliant models, Isabella and Emma. Johansson's Shoes in Gothenburg. Marks & Kattens for donating the yarn. Paulina Reijnst for working with the makeup and hair.

We've listed below the names of the creative artists who designed the rooms at the Icehotel in 2009–2010 where we photographed this book and at the ice church that was photographed from the outside.

Pillar Hall: Arne Bergh and Anders Eriksson, Sweden.

Art Svit 307: Icehotel Production & Building team, Sweden.

Reception: Sofi Ruotsalainen and Mikael Nille Nilsson, Sweden.

Ice church: Åke Larsson, Marjoleine Vonk and Marnius Vroom, Sweden and the Netherlands.

The Icehotel

AN ENVIRONMENTALLY FRIENDLY FAIRY-TALE WORLD

At the Icehotel in the Sami village of Jukkasjärvi, we experienced the most fantastic stay close to nature. It is the world's biggest ice hotel at 5,500 square meters and is built totally of snow and ice. During each winter season, about 50,000 people visit the hotel, mostly from abroad. The Icehotel has the Torne River as its source, and the hotel exists in harmony with the world around it. After every summer, artists from all around the world create and rebuild the hotel from scratch. It is a unique concept, created entirely from the perspective of being environmentally friendly.

Contents

Foreword

SNOW AND ICE WERE MY FIRST SOURCES OF INSPIRATION
for this knitting book. In my mind I created pictures of wood-
land spirits and ice princesses in the wintry landscape and icy
environment. The garments everyone wore, knitted with wool's
warmth and softness, would contrast against the Scandinavian
winter's snow crystals and cold.

Knitting with ecological wool was an obvious choice for me.
Using such a yarn, which is produced following strict rules,
I could help preserve the environment and, at the same time,
create a collection of the finest woolens.

My hope is you will feel as happy and inspired by the collection
as I felt as I created the pieces. The range of designs includes
simple garments for beginners as well as some that are a bit
more difficult for more experienced knitters. I also want to
share my tips and advice about knitting that I've learned during
my career as a knitting designer.

My imaginary world of ice princesses has been realized through
photographer Ewa K. Andinsson's fantastic pictures. Some
of the collection was photographed in one of Sweden's most
exotic tourist experiences, the Icehotel in Jukkasjärvi. It offers
an enchanted environment in which ice columns and ice crystal
crowns in the pillared hall shift from the iciest light blue to the
darkest petroleum blue.

This book has been a dream come true for me. I hope that it will
inspire you and give you many relaxing moments with knitting
in your lap.

Good luck!

Ingalill Johan

INGALILL JOHANSSON

Gallery

Ecological wool's wonderful texture brings out the best in structure, cable, and lace knitting. The colors in the collection are natural white, gray, and beige. The yarn is made with only natural colors of sheep's wool. We chose two weights of the yarn for the various garment styles in the collection.

In these designs, the tough meets the romantic.

Natural White

Instructions for Lace
Knit Top // SEE PAGE 42

Instructions for Ribbed Cap, Wrist Warmers, and Shoulder Wrap/Skirt // SEE PAGE 44

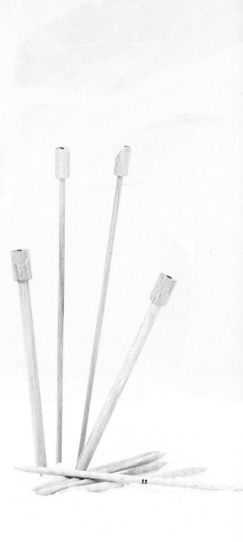

Instructions for Lace Knit Gloves,
Scarf, and Knee Socks // **SEE PAGE 47**

Instructions for Holey Top // SEE PAGE 52

Instructions for Lace
Sweater // SEE PAGE 56

Instructions for Short-Sleeve Bolero // SEE PAGE 61

Instructions for the Wrist Warmers and
Skirt // SEE PAGE 44

Left: instructions for Texture Knit Cardigan // SEE PAGE 65
Right: instructions for Texture Knit Vest // SEE PAGE 72

Gray

Instructions for Cabled Cap, Cowl, Wrist Warmers, and Knee Socks // **SEE PAGE 80**

Instructions for Coat with Relief
Stitch Borders // SEE PAGE 85

Instructions for Lace
Dress // SEE PAGE 100

Instructions for Stockinette Dress
with Garter Stitch Edgings and
Buttons // SEE PAGE 105

Instructions for Cabled
Cardigan // SEE PAGE 114

Instructions for Sweater with Relief
Stitch Borders // SEE PAGE 120

Beige

Instructions for Raglan Sweater with Placket // **SEE PAGE 126**

Instructions for Sweater
with Front Placket and
Pockets // SEE PAGE 131

Instructions for Lacy Sweater with
Ruffled Edges // **SEE PAGE 136**

Instructions for Gloves with
Ruffled Edges // **SEE PAGE 144**

Instructions for Short-Sleeve Vest (shown here with and without optional fringe) //
SEE PAGE 147

Instructions for Pleated Cap, Gloves, Leg
Warmers, and Neck Warmer // **SEE PAGE 151**

Instructions for Garter Stitch
Shawl // SEE PAGE 155

Knitting Patterns

Lace Knit Top

This pretty top goes just as well with a pair of jeans as a summer skirt. If you are a new knitter, this project will help build your skills. It is made in two straight pieces and sewn up the sides.

Photo page 10

finished measurements

33 (36½, 40½, 44, 48, 53)" (84 [92.5, 103, 112, 122, 134.5] cm) bust circumference and 21½ (23¾, 23¾, 26, 26, 28¼)" (54.5 [60.5, 60.5, 66, 66, 72] cm) long. To fit woman's sizes x-small (small, medium, large, 1X, 2X). Shown in size small.

yarn

Baby weight (fine #2).

Marks & Kattens Eco Baby Wool (100% wool; 91 yd [83 m]/25 g): natural white 173, 9 (10, 11, 12, 13, 14) balls.

needles

U.S. size 7 (4.5 mm) needles.

Adjust needle size if necessary to obtain the correct gauge.

notions

Locking markers (m) or safety pins; tapestry needle.

gauge

19 sts and 36 rows = 4" (10 cm) in garter st.

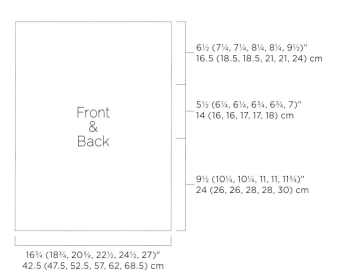

6½ (7¼, 7¼, 8¼, 8¼, 9½)"
16.5 (18.5, 18.5, 21, 21, 24) cm

5½ (6¼, 6¼, 6¾, 6¾, 7)"
14 (16, 16, 17, 17, 18) cm

Front
&
Back

9½ (10¼, 10¼, 11, 11, 11¾)"
24 (26, 26, 28, 28, 30) cm

16¾ (18¾, 20¾, 22½, 24½, 27)"
42.5 (47.5, 52.5, 57, 62, 68.5) cm

BACK

CO 80 (89, 98, 107, 116, 128) sts.

Rows 1–3: Knit.

Row 4: (RS) K3, *(yo) twice, sl 1, k2tog, psso; rep from * to last 2 sts, k2.

Row 5: K3, *(k1, p1) in double yo, k1; rep from * to last 2 sts, k2.

Rows 6–20: Knit.

Rep Rows 1–20 8 (9, 9, 10, 10, 11) more times, then rep Rows 1–8 once more; 10 (11, 11, 12, 12, 13) lace rows.

BO all sts loosely.

FRONT

Work same as for back.

FINISHING

Weave in ends. Block pieces to finished measurements. Place markers (pm) along side edge of both pieces, about 9½ (10¼, 10¼, 11, 11, 11¾)" (24 [26, 26, 28, 28, 30] cm) from bottom edge for side seam, then 5½ (6¼, 6¼, 6¾, 6¾, 7)" (14 [16, 16, 17, 17, 18] cm) above first markers for armhole.

With RS tog, and WS facing, sew side seams from bottom edge to first m. Leaving armholes open, beg at 2nd m and sew pieces tog for about 2" (5 cm). Turn with RS facing and sew rem seam to top edge. Fold the top part down for the collar.

Ribbed Cap, Wrist Warmers, and Shoulder Wrap/Skirt

Here's a warm, cozy, and easy-to-knit three-piece set. You can wear the shoulder wrap over a coat or as a skirt over a pair of tights or leggings.

Photos pages 11 and 15

finished measurements

CAP // 17¼" (44 cm) brim circumference and 10¼" (26 cm) long.

WRIST WARMERS // 8" (20.5 cm) hand circumference and 18¾" (47.5 cm) long.

SHOULDER WRAP/SKIRT // 19¾ (21¼, 22¾, 24½, 26, 27½)" (50 [54, 58, 62, 66, 70] cm) neck/waist circumference and 20 (20½, 20¾, 21¼, 21¾, 22)" (51 [52, 52.5, 54, 55, 56] cm) long. To fit woman's x-small (small, medium, large, 1X, 2X). Shown in size medium.

yarn

Worsted weight (medium #4).

Marks & Kattens Eco Wool (100% eco-wool; 88 yd [80 m]/50 g): natural white 1979, 2 balls for cap, 4 balls for wrist warmers, and 6 (6, 7, 7, 8, 8) balls for shoulder wrap/skirt.

needles

CAP // U.S. size 8 (5 mm): 16" (40 cm) long circular (cir). U.S. size 9 (5.5 mm): 16" (40 cm) long circular and set of 5 double-pointed needles (dpn).

WRIST WARMERS // U.S. size 9 (5.5 mm), set of 5 double-pointed needles (dpn).

SHOULDER WRAP/SKIRT // U.S. size 8 (5 mm): 24" (60 cm) long circular (cir) needle. U.S. size 9 (5.5 mm): 24" (60 cm) and 32" (80 cm) long circular needles.

Adjust needle sizes if necessary to obtain the correct gauge.

notions

Stitch marker (m); tapestry needle.

gauge

19½ sts and 22½ rows = 4" (10 cm) in k1, p3 rib on larger needles, unblocked.

22 sts and 23 rows = 4" (10 cm) in k1, p1 rib on larger needles, unblocked.

17 sts and 25 rows = 4" (10 cm) in k1, p4 rib on larger needles, blocked.

Change to double-pointed needles on the cap when there
are too few stitches to fit comfortably on the circular needle.
Likewise, change to the shorter circular needle on the shoulder
wrap/skirt when there are too few stitches to work comfortably
on the longer circular needle.

CAP

With smaller cir needle, CO 84 sts and join, being careful not to
twist sts. Place marker (pm) for beg of rnd. Work in k1, k1 rib for
5 rnds.

Change to larger cir needle.

Rnd 1: *K1, p3; rep from * around.

Rep Rnd 1 until cap measures 8½" (21.5 cm) from cast-on edge.

Shape top

Next (dec) rnd: *K1, p2tog, p1; rep from * around—63 sts.

Work 5 rnds even.

Next (dec) rnd: *K1, p2tog; rep from * around—42 sts.

Work 2 rnds even.

Next (dec) rnd: *K2tog; rep from * around—21 sts.

Next (dec) rnd: *K2tog; rep from * to last st, k1—11 sts.

Cut yarn, draw tail through rem sts, and pull tight to secure.

Weave in ends.

WRIST WARMERS (make 2)

CO 48 sts onto one dpn. Divide sts evenly over 4 dpns (12 sts
on each dpn) and join, being careful not to twist sts. Pm for beg
of rnd.

Work in k1, p1 rib until piece measures 11¾" (30 cm).

Next (dec) rnd: *K3tog, work 9 sts in est rib patt to end of
needle; rep from * 3 more times—40 sts. Work even until piece
measures 14¼" (36 cm).

Next (inc) rnd: *Knit into (front, back, front) of next st, work
9 sts in est rib patt to end of needle; rep from * 3 more
times—48 sts. Work even until piece measures 17" (43 cm) long,
ending 5 sts before end of last rnd.

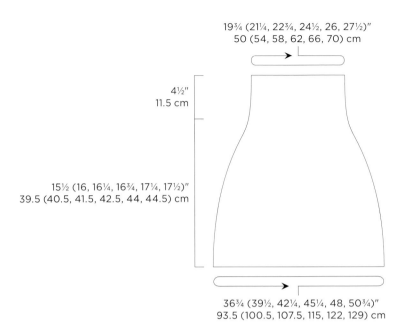

19¾ (21¼, 22¾, 24½, 26, 27½)"
50 (54, 58, 62, 66, 70) cm

4½"
11.5 cm

15½ (16, 16¼, 16¾, 17¼, 17½)"
39.5 (40.5, 41.5, 42.5, 44, 44.5) cm

36¾ (39½, 42¼, 45¼, 48, 50¾)"
93.5 (100.5, 107.5, 115, 122, 129) cm

THUMB

BO last 5 sts of rnd and first 5 sts of next rnd, work in rib patt to end over rem sts—38 sts.

Next rnd: CO 2 sts over thumb gap—40 sts.

Work even in rib patt until piece measures 18½" (47 cm). BO loosely in rib. Weave in ends.

SHOULDER WRAP/SKIRT

With longer cir needle, CO 156 (168, 180, 192, 204, 216) sts and join, being careful not to twist sts. Pm for beg of rnd.

Rnd 1: *K1, p5; rep from * around. Work even until piece measures 4½ (5, 5¼, 5¾, 6, 6½)" (11.5 [12.5, 13.5, 14.5, 15, 16.5] cm) from beg.

Next (dec) rnd: *K1, p2tog, p3, k1, p5; rep from * around—143 (154, 165, 176, 187, 198) sts. Work even until piece measures 7½ (7¾, 8¼, 8¾, 9, 9½)" (19 [19.5, 21, 22, 23, 24] cm from beg.

Next (dec) rnd: *K1, p4, k1, p2tog, p3; rep from * around—130 (140, 150, 160, 170, 180) sts.

Work even until piece measures 10¼ (10¾, 11, 11½, 11¾, 12¼)" (26 [27.5, 28, 29, 30, 31] cm) from beg.

Next (dec) rnd: *K1, p2tog, p2, k1, p4; rep from * around—117 (126, 135, 144, 153, 162) sts. Work even until piece measures 13 (13½, 13¾, 14¼, 14½, 15)" (33 [34.5, 35, 36, 37, 38] cm) from beg.

Next (dec) rnd: *K1, p3, k1, p2tog, p2; rep from * around—104 (112, 120, 128, 136, 144) sts. Work even until piece measures 15½ (16, 16¼, 16¾, 17¼, 17½)" (39.5 [40.5, 41.5, 42.5, 44, 44.5] cm) from beg.

Change to smaller cir needle. Work in k1, p1 rib for 4¼" (11 cm). BO loosely in rib.

FINISHING

Weave in ends. Block to finished measurements.

Lace Knit Gloves, Scarf, and Knee Socks

This is a sweetly romantic three-piece set. The lace knitting has many fine details including a pretty crocheted finish along the edges.

Photo page 12

finished measurements

GLOVES // 9 (9¼)" (23 [23.5] cm) hand circumference and 10¾ (11)" (27.5 [28] cm) long, with cuff folded. Shown in size 9" (23 cm) circumference.

SCARF // About 8¾" (22 cm) wide and 46½" (118 cm) long.

KNEE SOCKS // 8¼ (9, 9¼)" (21 [23, 23.5] cm) foot circumference and 16¾ (17½, 18¼)" (42.5 [44.5, 46.5] cm) long to heel. Shown in size 9" (23 cm) circumference.

yarn

Baby weight (fine #2).

Marks & Kattens Eco Baby Wool (100% eco-wool; 91 yd [83 m]/25 g): natural white 173, 5 (5) balls for gloves, 5 balls for scarf, and 7 (8, 9) balls for knee socks.

needles

GLOVES // U.S. size 2.5 (3 mm): set of 5 double-pointed needles (dpn).

SCARF // U.S. size 6 (4 mm) needles.

KNEE SOCKS // U.S. size 1.5 (2.5 mm): set of 5 double-pointed needles (dpn). U.S. size 2.5 (3 mm): set of 5 double-pointed needles (dpn).

Adjust needle sizes if necessary to obtain the correct gauge.

notions

U.S. size D-3 (3.25 mm) crochet hook; stitch markers; tapestry needle.

gauge

26 sts and 37 rows = 4" (10 cm) in St st on U.S. size 2.5 (3 mm) needles.

21 sts and 32½ rows = 4" (10 cm) in Lace Patt on U.S. size 6 (4 mm) needles.

STITCH GUIDE

Shell Edging (multiple of 4 sts)

Rnd 1: Ch 4, *skip 1 sc, 1 dc in next sc, ch 1; rep from * around, ending with 1 sl st in the 3rd ch of 4-ch at beg of rnd.

Rnd 2: Ch 3, 4 dc in first ch-loop, *1 sc in next ch-loop, 5 dc in next ch-loop; rep from * around. Fasten off.

GLOVES
Right glove

With size 2.5 (3 mm) dpns, CO 56 (56) sts. Divide sts evenly over 4 dpns, with 14 (14) sts on each needle. Join to work in the rnd, being careful not to twist sts. Place marker (pm) for beg of rnd.

Purl 1 rnd. Knit 2 rnds. Work 16 rnds of Patt 1 chart. Knit 4 rnds and inc 2 (4) sts evenly spaced across last rnd—58 (60) sts.

Turn piece with WS out. Change to St st (knit every rnd) until piece measures 5½ (6)" (14 [15] cm) from where work was turned.

Next rnd: K9 sts with a piece of contrasting waste yarn, sl sts just knit back to left needle and knit again with main yarn, knit to end. Continue even until piece measures 7½ (7¾)" (19 [20] cm) from where work was turned.

INDEX FINGER

Knit first 8 (8) sts, CO 1 st, place next 42 (44) sts onto holders, knit last 8 (8) sts—17 (17) sts. Distribute sts evenly over 3 dpns. Join to work in the rnd. Pm for beg of rnd. Work in St st until finger measures 2¾ (3)" (7 [7.5] cm).

Next (dec) rnd: (K2tog) 8 times, k1—9 sts.

Knit 1 rnd even.

Rep dec rnd once more—5 sts. Cut yarn, draw tail through rem sts, and pull tight to secure.

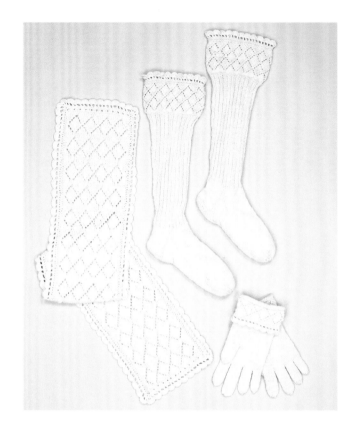

MIDDLE FINGER

Place first 8 (8) sts and last 8 (8) sts onto dpns, leave rem 26 (28) sts on holders. Join yarn, pick up and knit 1 (2) st(s) in CO st at base of index finger, k8 (8), CO 1 (1) st, k8 (8)—18 (19) sts. Distribute sts evenly over 3 dpns. Pm for beg of rnd. Work in St st until finger measures 3⅛ (3¼)" (8 [8.5] cm).

Next (dec) rnd: (K2tog) 9 times, k0 (1)—9 (10) sts.

Knit 1 rnd even.

Next (dec) rnd: (K2tog) 4 (5) times, k1 (0)—5 sts. Cut yarn, draw tail through rem sts, and pull tight to secure.

RING FINGER

Place first 7 (8) sts and last 7 (8) sts onto dpns, leaving rem 12 (12) sts on holders. Join yarn, pick up and knit 1 (0) st in base of

CO st at base of middle finger, k7 (8), CO 1 (0) st, k7 (8)—16 (16) sts. Distribute sts evenly over 3 dpns. Pm for beg of rnd. Work in St st until finger measures 2¾ (3)" (7 [7.5] cm).

Next (dec) rnd: (K2tog) 8 (8) times—8 (8) sts.

Knit 1 rnd even.

Next (dec) rnd: (K2tog) 4 (4) times—4 (4) sts. Cut yarn, draw tail through rem sts, and pull tight to secure.

LITTLE FINGER
Place rem 12 (12) sts onto dpns. Join yarn, pick up and knit 2 sts at base of ring finger—14 (14) sts. Evenly distribute sts over 3 dpns. Join to work in the rnd. Pm for beg fo rnd. Work in St st until finger measures 2 (2¼)" (5 [5.5] cm).

Next (dec) rnd: (K2tog) 7 (7) times—7 (7) sts.

Knit 1 rnd even.

Next (dec) rnd: (K2tog) 3 (3) times, k1 (1)—4 (4) sts. Cut yarn, draw tail through rem sts, and pull tight to secure.

THUMB
Remove waste yarn from thumb and arrange the revealed 18 (18) sts over 3 dpns and pick up 1 st at each side of opening—20 (20) sts. Join to work in the rnd. Pm for beg of rnd. Work in St st for 2 (2¼)" (5 [5.5] cm).

Next (dec) rnd: (K2tog) 10 (10) times—10 (10) sts.

Knit 1 rnd even.

Next (dec) rnd: (K2tog) 5 (5) times—5 (5) sts. Cut yarn, draw tail through rem sts, and pull tight to secure.

Left glove
Work left glove as for right until piece measures 5½ (6)" (14 [15] cm) from where work was turned.

Next rnd: Knit to last 9 (9) sts, knit the last 9 (9) sts with a piece of contrasting waste yarn for thumb opening, sl sts just knit back to left needle and knit again with main yarn.

Continue same as for right glove.

Finishing
CROCHET EDGING
With crochet hook and RS of cuff facing, join yarn to cast-on edge with a sl st in a cast-on st, ch 1, work sc around, with 1 sc in each knit st, ending with 1 sl st in ch at beg of rnd. Work Shell Edging. Weave in ends. Fold cuffs to RS.

SCARF
With size 6 (4 mm) needles, CO 38 sts. Knit 1 WS row.

Next row: (RS) K2, *yo, ssk, k1; rep from * to end.

Next (inc) row: (WS) Knit and inc 1 st—39 sts.

Next row: (RS) Knit.

Next row: K3 (edge sts), purl to last sts, k3 (edge sts).

Rep last 2 rows once more.

***Next row:** (RS) K3 (edge sts), work Row 1 of Patt 2 chart over next 33 sts, k3 (edge sts).

Next row: K3 (edge sts), work Row 2 of Patt 2 chart over next 33 sts, k3 (edge sts).

Work Rows 3–16 of chart as est. Work 4 rows of St st, keeping edge sts in garter st (knit every row). Rep from * 17 more times. Knit 1 row.

Next (dec) row: (WS) Knit and dec 1 st—38 sts.

Next row: (RS) K2, *yo, ssk, k1; rep from * to end.

Knit 1 row. BO all sts loosely.

Finishing
CROCHET EDGING
With crochet hook and RS facing, join yarn to cast-on edge with a sl st in one edge, ch 1, work sc around, with 1 sc in each knit st, and 3 sc in each corner, 1 sc in every other row along side edges, ending with 1 sl st in ch at beg of rnd.

Work Shell Edging, working (1 dc, ch 1, 1 dc, ch 1, 1 dc) in each corner of Rnd 1.

Pattern 1, gloves

- ☐ k on RS; p on WS
- ⊙ yo
- ☑ k2tog
- ☒ ssk
- ⋋ sl 1, k2tog, psso
- ☐ pattern repeat

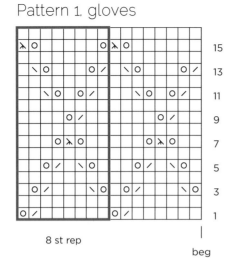

8 st rep

beg

Pattern 2, scarf

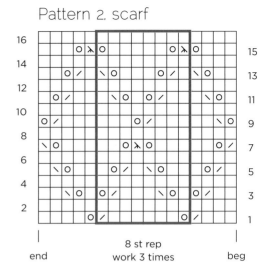

end   8 st rep
       work 3 times   beg

KNEE SOCKS (make 2)

With size 2.5 (3 mm) dpns, CO 80 (88, 96) sts. Divide sts evenly over 4 dpn, with 20 (22, 24) sts on each needle. Join to work in the rnd, being careful not to twist sts. Place marker (pm) for beg of rnd; rnds beg at center back.

(Purl 1 rnd, knit 1 rnd) 3 times.

Work 32 rnds of Patt 3 chart. Knit 4 rnds.

Change to size 1.5 (2.5 mm) dpns.

Next rnd: K1, *p2, k2; rep from * to last st, k1.

Continue in rib until leg measures 5½" (14 cm) from beg.

Dec rnd 1: K1, p2tog, *k2, p2; rep from * to last 5 sts, k2, ssp, k1—2 sts dec'd.

Work 7 rnds even.

Dec rnd 2: K1, k2tog, k1, *p2, k2; rep from * to last 6 sts, p2, k1, ssk, k1—2 sts dec'd.

Work 7 rnds even.

Dec rnd 3: K1, k2tog, *p2, k2; rep from * to last 5 sts, p2, ssk, k1—2 sts dec'd.

Work 7 rnds even.

Dec rnd 4: K1, p2tog, p1, *k2, p2; rep from * to last 6 sts, k2, p1, ssp, k1—2 sts dec'd.

Rep dec rnd every 8 rnds 2 (3, 4) more times, then every 4 rnds 4 times, continuing sequence Dec rnd 1, Dec rnd 2, Dec rnd 3, then Dec rnd 4—60 (66, 72) sts rem.

Work even until leg measures 14¼ (15, 15¾)" (36 [38, 40] cm).

Change to size 2.5 (3 mm) dpns and St st (knit every rnd). Knit 2 rnds and dec 4 (6, 10) sts evenly spaced on first rnd—56 (60, 62) sts. Redistribute sts with 14 (15, 15) sts each on Needles 1 and 3 and 14 (15, 16) sts each on Needles 2 and 4.

Heel

Knit to end of Needle 1 and dec 1 st, turn. Purl sts from Needle 1, then purl sts from Needle 4—27 (29, 30) sts. Continue over Needles 1 and 4 only, work 19 (21, 21) more rows of St st.

Next row: (WS) Purl and inc 1 st on Needle 1—28 (30, 31) sts.

Pattern 3, socks

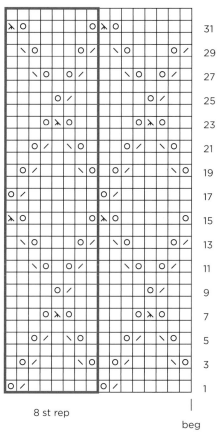

8 st rep

beg

- ☐ k on RS; p on WS
- ⊡ yo
- ⟋ k2tog
- ⟍ ssk
- ⋏ sl 1, k2tog, psso
- ▢ pattern repeat

Next row: (RS) K18 (19, 19) sts, ssk, k1; turn.

Row 2: (WS) Sl 1, p9 (9, 8) sts, p2tog, p1; turn.

Row 3: Sl 1, k9 (9, 8) sts, ssk, k1; turn.

Row 4: Sl 1, p9 (9, 8) sts, p2tog, p1; turn.

Rep Rows 3 and 4 until all heel sts have been used up—12 (12, 11) sts rem.

Next row: (RS) Needle 4, knit 6 heel sts; Needle 1, knit 6 (6, 5) heel sts, then pick up and k13 (14, 15) sts along right side of heel flap; Needles 2 and 3, knit; Needle 4, pick up and k13 (14, 15) sts along left side of heel flap, knit 6 heel sts—66 (70, 72) sts. Join to work in the rnd. Pm for beg of rnd.

Knit 1 rnd.

Next (dec) rnd: Needle 1, knit to last 2 sts, k2tog, Needles 2 and 3, knit; Needle 4 ssk, then knit to end—2 sts dec'd.

Rep dec rnd every other rnd 5 more times—54 (58, 60) sts rem. Divide rem sts evenly over 4 dpns. Continue even in St st until foot measures 7¾ (8¼, 8¾)″ (20 [21, 22] cm) from heel.

Shape toe

Next (dec) rnd: Needle 1, knit to last 3 sts, ssk, k1; Needle 2, k1, k2tog; Needle 3, knit to last 3 sts, ssk, k1; Needle 4, k1, k2tog, knit to end—4 sts dec'd.

Rep dec rnd every other rnd 5 (6, 6) more times, then every rnd 4 (4, 5) times—14 (14, 12) sts.

Next (dec) rnd: (K2tog) 7, 7, 6 times—7 (7, 6) sts rem. Cut yarn, draw tail through rem sts, and pull tight to secure.

Finishing

CROCHET EDGING

With crochet hook, join yarn to cast-on edge with a sl st in a cast-on st, ch 1, work sc around, with 1 sc in each knit st, ending with 1 sl st in ch at beg of rnd. Work Shell Edging.

Weave in ends.

Holey Top

Notable for its raw edges and extreme holes, this top looks harder to make than it is. If you can knit, purl, and bind off, then it will be a breeze.

Photo page 13

finished measurements

39 (42½, 46½, 49½, 53, 57½)" (99 [108, 118, 125.5, 134.5, 146] cm bust circumference and about 19 (19¾, 20½, 21¼, 22, 22¾)" (48 [50, 52, 54, 56, 58] cm) long. To fit woman's sizes x-small (small, medium, large, 1X, 2X). Shown in size medium.

yarn

Worsted weight (medium #4).

Marks & Kattens Eco Wool (100% eco-wool; 88 yd [80 m]/50 g): natural white 1979, 10 (11, 12, 13, 14, 15) balls.

needles

U.S. size 10½ (6.5 mm) needles.

Adjust needle size if necessary to obtain the correct gauge.

notions

Two stitch holders; tapestry needle.

gauge

14½ sts and 20 rows = 4" (10 cm) in St st.

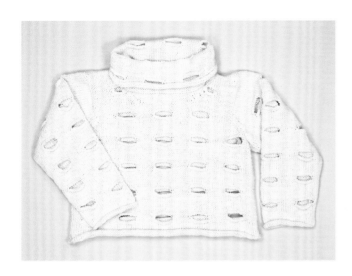

Rep Rows 16–29 throughout. **Note:** After shaping the armholes, work only 3 sets of holes in each rep.

Work even until piece measures 11 (11½, 11¾, 12¼, 12¾, 13)" (28 [29, 30, 31, 32, 33] cm) from beg, ending with a WS row.

Shape armholes

BO 6 (6, 7, 7, 7, 7) sts at beg of next 2 rows—61 (67, 72, 78, 84, 92) sts.

Next (dec) row: (RS) K1 (edge st), k2tog, knit to last 3 sts, ssk, k1 (edge st)—2 sts dec'd.

Rep dec row every RS row 4 more times—51 (57, 62, 68, 74, 82) sts.

Continue even in patt until armhole measures 7¼ (7½, 7¾, 8¼, 8¾, 9)" (18.5 [19, 20, 21, 22, 23] cm), ending with a WS row.

Shape neck

Next row: (RS) Work 15 (18, 19, 22, 25, 29) sts, place center 21 (21, 24, 24, 24, 24) sts onto a st holder for back neck, join a second ball of yarn and work rem 15 (18, 19, 22, 25, 29) sts. Continue each side separately. BO every other row at neck edge 1 st twice—13 (16, 17, 20, 23, 27) sts rem each side. BO rem sts.

FRONT

Work front as for back until armhole measures 3¼ (3½, 4, 4¼, 4¾, 5)" (8.5 [9, 10, 11, 12, 12.5] cm), ending with a WS row.

Next row: Work 19 (22, 24, 26, 29, 33) sts, place center 13 (13, 16, 16, 16, 16) sts onto st holder for front neck, join a second ball of yarn and work rem 19 (22, 24, 26, 29, 33) sts. Continue each side separately.

BO every other row at each neck edge 2 sts twice, then 1 st twice—13 (16, 18, 20, 23, 27) sts rem each side. Work even until armhole measures 8 (8¼, 8¾, 9, 9½, 9¾)" (20.5 [21, 22, 23, 24, 25] cm). BO rem sts.

Note

Only three sets of holes are worked for each repeat on the sleeves. Make sure to bind off stitches in the same place each time; if necessary, place stitch markers for the first and third sets of bound-off stitches after the first repeat to make sure the holes line up correctly.

BACK

CO 73 (79, 86, 92, 98, 106) sts.

Row 1: (WS) K1 (edge st), purl to last st, k1 (edge st).

Row 2: Knit.

Rep Rows 1 and 2 six more times, then rep Row 1 once more.

Row 16: (RS) K1 (edge st), k4 (7, 6, 9, 12, 16), *BO 7 (7, 8, 8, 8, 8) sts, k7 (7, 8, 8, 8, 8); rep from * 3 more times, BO 7 (7, 8, 8, 8, 8) sts, k4 (7, 6, 9, 12, 16), k1 (edge st).

Row 17: K1 (edge st), p4 (7, 6, 9, 12, 16), *CO 7 (7, 8, 8, 8, 8) sts, p7 (7, 8, 8, 8, 8)*; rep from * 3 more times, CO 7 (7, 8, 8, 8, 8) sts, p4 (7, 6, 9, 12, 16), k1 (edge st).

Rows 18–29: Rep Row 2 once, then rep Rows 1 and 2 five more times, then rep Row 1 once more.

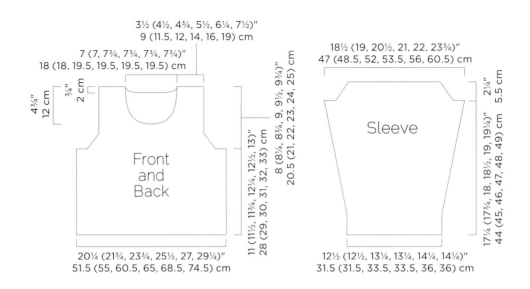

3½ (4½, 4¾, 5½, 6¼, 7½)"
9 (11.5, 12, 14, 16, 19) cm

7 (7, 7¾, 7¾, 7¾, 7¾)"
18 (18, 19.5, 19.5, 19.5, 19.5) cm

4¾" / 12 cm

¾" / 2 cm

Front and Back

11 (11½, 11¾, 12¼, 12½, 13)"
28 (29, 30, 31, 32, 33) cm

8 (8¼, 8¾, 9, 9½, 9¾)"
20.5 (21, 22, 23, 24, 25) cm

20¼ (21¾, 23¾, 25½, 27, 29¼)"
51.5 (55, 60.5, 65, 68.5, 74.5) cm

18½ (19, 20½, 21, 22, 23¾)"
47 (48.5, 52, 53.5, 56, 60.5) cm

Sleeve

2¼" / 5.5 cm

17¼ (17¾, 18, 18½, 19, 19¼)"
44 (45, 46, 47, 48, 49) cm

12½ (12½, 13¼, 13¼, 14¼, 14¼)"
31.5 (31.5, 33.5, 33.5, 36, 36) cm

Sleeves (make 2)

CO 45 (45, 48, 48, 52, 52) sts.

Row 1: (WS) K1 (edge st), purl to last st, k1 (edge st).

Row 2: Knit.

Rep Rows 1 and 2 five more times, then rep Row 1 once more.

Row 14: K1 (edge st), M1, knit to last st, M1, k1 (edge st)—2 sts inc'd. Rep inc row every 4 rows 0 (0, 0, 4, 2, 10) times, then every 6 rows 10 (11, 12, 9, 11, 6) times—67 (69, 74, 76, 80, 86) sts. Work new sts in St st and AT SAME TIME, continue patt as foll:

Row 15: Rep Row 1.

Row 16: (RS) K1 (edge st), k5 (5, 4, 4, 6, 6), *BO 7 (7, 8, 8, 8, 8) sts, k7 (7, 8, 8, 8, 8); rep from * once more, BO 7 (7, 8, 8, 8, 8) sts, k5 (5, 4, 4, 6, 6), k1 (edge st).

Row 17: K1 (edge st), p5 (5, 4, 4, 6, 6), *CO 7 (7, 8, 8, 8, 8) sts, p7 (7, 8, 8, 8, 8); rep from * once more, CO 7 (7, 8, 8, 8, 8) sts, p5 (5, 4, 4, 6, 6), k1 (edge st).

Rows 18–29: Rep Row 2 once, then rep Rows 1 and 2 five more times, then rep Row 1 once more.

Rep Rows 16–29 throughout. When inc are complete, work even until piece measures 17¼ (17¾, 18, 18½, 19, 19¼)" (44 [45, 46, 47, 48, 49] cm) from beg, ending with a WS row.

Shape cap

BO 6 (6, 7, 7, 7, 7) sts at beg of next 2 rows—55 (57, 60, 62, 66, 72) sts.

Next (dec) row: (RS) K1 (edge st), k2tog, work to last 3 sts, ssk, k1 (edge st)—2 sts dec'd.

Rep dec row every RS row 4 more times—45 (47, 50, 52, 56, 62) sts. BO rem sts loosely.

FINISHING

Weave in ends. Block pieces to finished measurements.

Sew right shoulder seam.

Collar

With RS facing, pick up and knit 22 (22, 24, 24, 24, 24) sts along left front neck, k13 (13, 16, 16, 16, 16) from front holder, pick up and k26 (26, 29, 29, 29, 29) sts along right neck edge, k21 (21, 24, 24, 24, 24) sts from back holder, pick up and k4 (4, 5, 5, 5, 5) sts along left back neck—86 (86, 98, 98, 98, 98) sts.

Row 1: (WS) K1 (edge st), purl to last st, k1 (edge st).

Row 2: Knit.

Rows 3–5: Rep Rows 1 and 2 once, then rep Row 1 once more.

Row 6: (RS) K1 (edge st), purl to last st, k1 (edge st).

Row 7: Knit.

Rows 8–20: Rep Rows 6 and 7 six more times, then rep Row 6 once more.

Row 21: (WS) K1 (edge st), *BO 7 (7, 8, 8, 8, 8) sts, k7 (7, 8, 8, 8, 8); rep from * to last st, k1 (edge st).

Row 22: K1 (edge st), *p7 (7, 8, 8, 8, 8), CO 7 (7, 8, 8, 8, 8) sts; rep from * to last st, k1 (edge st).

Rows 23–34: Rep Row 7 once, rep Rows 6 and 7 five times, then rep Row 6 once more.

Rows 35 and 36: Rep Rows 21 and 22 once more.

Rows 37–42: Rep Row 7 once, rep Rows 6 and 7 twice, then rep Row 6 once more.

BO all sts loosely.

Sew left shoulder seam and about 1″ (2.5 cm) of collar seam with seam at WS. Turn piece with WS facing, complete turtleneck seam with seam at RS of body; seam will not show when collar is folded down.

Sew in sleeves. Sew side and sleeve seams.

Lace Sweater

Gossamer lace patterns border this flattering long sweater. This style looks good on almost everyone, and the sweater is as nice for parties as for everyday.

Photo page 14

finished measurements

29 (32, 35, 38½, 42¼, 46½)" (73.5 [81.5, 89, 98, 107.5, 118] cm) bust circumference and 28½ (29¼, 30, 30¾, 31¾, 32½)" (72.5 [74.5, 76, 78, 80.5, 82.5] cm) long. To fit woman's sizes x-small (small, medium, large, 1X, 2X). Shown in size medium.

yarn

Baby weight (fine #2).

Marks & Kattens Eco Baby Wool (100% eco-wool; 91 yd [83 m]/25 g): natural white 173, 18 (19, 20, 22, 24, 26) balls.

needles

U.S. size 4 (3.5) needles.

U.S. size 6 (4 mm) needles.

Adjust needle sizes if necessary to obtain the correct gauge.

notions

U.S. size D-3 (3 mm) crochet hook; stitch holders; tapestry needle.

gauge

22 sts and 31 rows = 4" (10 cm) in St st on larger needles.

27 sts and 39 rows = 4" (10 cm) in Patt 1 on larger needles.

24 sts and 32 rows = 4" (10 cm) in Patt 3 on larger needles.

Work Rows 3–12 of Patt 1, then rep Rows 1–12 four more times. AT THE SAME TIME, dec 1 st every 6 (6, 6, 8, 8, 8) rows 16 (16, 16, 15, 15, 15) times as foll: K1 (edge st), k2tog, work in est patt to last 3 sts, ssk, k1 (edge st)—93 (101, 109, 121, 131, 143) sts.

When 60 rows of Patt 1 chart have been worked (5 rep), change to smaller needles. Knit 6 rows, work 8 rows of Patt 2, then knit 6 rows and continue dec at sides as est.

Change to larger needles.

Next row: (RS) K1 (edge st), beg at your size on right side of Patt 3 chart and work 3 (2, 1, 4, 4, 5) st(s), rep next 10 sts 9 (10, 11, 12, 13, 14) times, work rem 4 (3, 2, 5, 5, 6) sts of chart, k1 (edge st).

Next row: K1 (edge st), beg at left side of Patt 3 chart and work 4 (3, 2, 5, 5, 6) sts, rep next 10 sts 9 (10, 11, 12, 13, 14) times, work rem 3 (2, 1, 4, 4, 5) st(s) of chart, k1 (edge st).

Work Rows 3–16 of Patt 3, then rep Rows 1–16 until piece measures 15¾ (16¼, 16¼, 16½, 16½, 17)″ (40 [41, 41, 42, 42, 43] cm) from beg, ending with a WS row.

Change to smaller needles.

Next (dec) row: (RS), K1 (edge st), k4 (8, 2, 3, 8, 3), *k2tog, k2 (2, 3, 3, 3, 4); rep from * 19 (19, 19, 21, 21, 21) more times, k2tog, knit to end—72 (80, 88, 98, 108, 120) sts. Knit 5 rows even.

Change to larger needles.

Next (inc) row: (RS) K1 (edge st), M1, knit to last st, M1, k1 (edge st)—2 sts inc'd.

Next row: K1 (edge st), purl to last st, k1 (edge st).

Continue in St st as est and AT THE SAME TIME, rep inc row every 8 rows 4 more times—82 (90, 98, 108, 118, 130) sts.

Work even until piece measures 21¼ (21¾, 22, 22½, 22¾, 23¼)″ (54 [55, 56, 57, 58, 59] cm) from beg, ending with a WS row.

Shape armholes

BO 5 (7, 8, 10, 12, 15) sts at beg of next 2 rows, 3 sts at beg of next 0 (0, 0, 0, 2, 2) rows, 2 sts at beg of next 2 (2, 2, 4, 2, 2) rows, then 1 st at beg of next 4 (4, 6, 4, 4, 6) rows—64 (68, 72, 76, 80, 84) sts.

Notes

When increasing or decreasing over lace patterns, if a yarnover cannot be worked with its accompanying decrease (k2tog or ssk), work that stitch in stockinette.

BACK

With larger needles, CO 125 (133, 141, 151, 161, 173) sts. Knit 1 WS row.

Next row: (RS) K1 (edge st), beg at your size on right side of Patt 1 chart and work 13 (3, 7, 12, 3, 9) sts, rep next 14 sts 7 (9, 9, 9, 11, 11) times, work rem 12 (2, 6, 11, 2, 8) sts of chart, k1 (edge st).

Next row: K1 (edge st), beg at left side of Patt 1 chart and work 12 (2, 6, 11, 2, 8) sts, rep next 14 sts 7 (9, 9, 9, 11, 11) times, work rem 13 (3, 7, 12, 3, 9) sts of chart, k1 (edge st).

Pattern 1

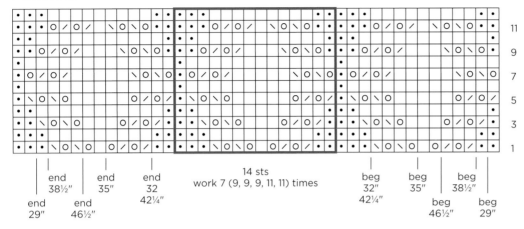

end
29"

end
38½"

end
46½"

end
35"

end
32
42¼"

14 sts
work 7 (9, 9, 11, 11) times

beg
32"
42¼"

beg
35"

beg
46½"

beg
38½"

beg
29"

Pattern 2

3

1

☐ k on RS; p on WS

• p on RS; k on WS

O yo

╱ k2tog

╲ ssk

☐ pattern repeat

Pattern 3, body

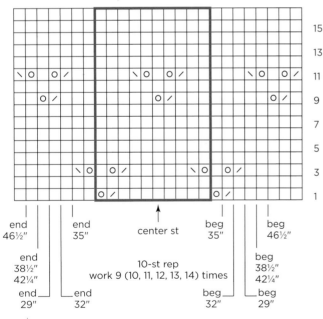

15

13

11

9

7

5

3

1

end
46½"

end
38½"
42¼"

end
29"

end
35"

end
32"

center st

10-st rep
work 9 (10, 11, 12, 13, 14) times

beg
35"

beg
32"

beg
38½"
42¼"

beg
29"

beg
46½"

Pattern 3, sleeve

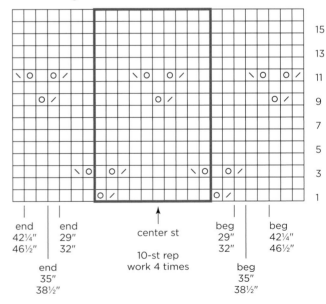

15

13

11

9

7

5

3

1

end
42¼"
46½"

end
35"
38½"

end
29"

end
32"

center st

10-st rep
work 4 times

beg
29"

beg
35"
38½"

beg
32"

beg
42¼"
46½"

Work even until armhole measures 6¾ (7, 7½, 7¾, 8¼, 8¾)" (17 [18, 19, 20, 21, 22] cm), ending with a WS row.

Shape shoulders and neck

Next row: (RS) BO 5 (6, 6, 7, 7, 8) sts, k11 (12, 13, 14, 15, 16), place center 32 (32, 34, 34, 36, 36) sts onto holder for neck, join a second ball of yarn and knit to end.

Next row: BO 5 (6, 6, 7, 7, 8) sts, purl to last 2 sts of left shoulder, p2tog; on other side, BO 1 st, purl to end.

Next row: BO 5 (5, 6, 6, 7, 7) sts, knit to last 2 sts of right shoulder, k2tog; on other side, BO 1 st, knit to end.

Next row: BO 5 (5, 6, 6, 7, 7) sts, purl to neck; on other side, purl to end.

BO 4 (5, 5, 6, 6, 7) sts at the beg of next 2 rows.

FRONT

Work front as for back until piece measures 21¼ (21¾, 22, 22½, 22¾, 23¼)" (54 [55, 56, 57, 58, 59] cm) from beg, ending with a WS row. Place marker (pm) onto each side of center 4 sts.

Shape armholes

BO 5 (7, 8, 10, 12, 15) sts at beg of next 2 rows, 3 sts at beg of next 0 (0, 0, 0, 2, 2) rows, 2 sts at beg of next 2 (2, 2, 4, 2, 2) rows, then 1 st at beg of next 4 (4, 6, 4, 4, 6) rows. AT THE SAME TIME, when armhole measures 0 (½, ½, ¾, ¾, 1¼)" (0 [1, 1, 2, 2, 3] cm), place center 4 sts onto holder for neck and join a second ball of yarn to work each side of front separately, and CO 1 st at neck edge; knit this new st every row for edge st—31 (33, 35, 37, 39, 41) sts rem each side when armhole shaping is complete.

Work even until armhole measures 2¾ (3¼, 3¼, 3½, 4, 4¼)" (7 [8, 8, 9, 10, 11] cm), ending with a WS row.

Shape neck

BO every other row at neck edge 11 (11, 12, 12, 13, 13) sts once, 2 sts twice, then 1 st twice—14 (16, 17, 19, 20, 22) sts rem. Work even until armhole measures 6¾ (7, 7½, 7¾, 8¼, 8¾)" (17 [18, 19, 20, 21, 22] cm), ending with a WS row.

Shape shoulders

BO 8 sts at beg of next 0 (0, 0, 0, 0, 2) rows, 7 sts at beg of next 0 (0, 0, 2, 4, 4) rows, 6 sts at beg of next 0 (2, 4, 4, 2, 0) rows, 5 sts at beg of next 4 (4, 2, 0, 0, 0) rows, then 4 sts at beg of next 2 (0, 0, 0, 0, 0) rows.

SLEEVES

With smaller needles, CO 58 (58, 60, 60, 64, 64) sts. Knit 5 rows.

Next row: (RS) K1 (edge st), work Row 1 of Patt 2 to last st, k1 (edge st).

Next row: K1 (edge st), work Row 2 of Patt 2 to last st, k1 (edge st).

Continue in Patt 2 as est for 6 more rows. Knit 5 rows.

Next (dec) row: K1 (edge st) k1 (1, 3, 3, 5, 5), *k2tog, k3; rep from * 10 more times, k0 (0, 0, 0, 2, 2), k1 (edge st)—47 (47, 49, 49, 53, 53) sts.

Change to larger needles.

Next row: (RS) K1 (edge st), beg your size at right side of Patt 3 chart, work 2 (2, 3, 3, 5, 5) sts, rep next 10 sts 4 times, work rem 3 (3, 4, 4, 6, 6) sts of chart, k1 (edge st).

Next row: K1 (edge st), beg at left side of Patt 3 chart, work 3 (3, 4, 4, 6, 6) sts, rep next 10 sts 4 times, work rem 2 (2, 3, 3, 5, 5) sts of chart, k1 (edge st).

Continue in patt as est and AT THE SAME TIME, when piece measures 4¾" (12 cm) from beg, inc 1 st each end of next row as foll: K1 (edge st), M1, work as est to last st, M1, k1 (edge st)—2 sts inc'd.

Rep inc row every 12 (10, 10, 8, 8, 8) rows 7 (9, 5, 12, 12, 7) times, then every 0 (0, 8, 0, 0, 6) rows 0 (0, 5, 0, 0, 7) times—63 (67, 71, 75, 79, 83) sts. Work new sts into patt.

Work even until piece measures 16½ (17, 17¼, 17¾, 18, 18½)" (42 [43, 44, 45, 46, 47] cm) from beg, ending with a WS row.

Shape cap

BO 6 (7, 8, 9, 10, 12) sts at beg of next 2 rows, then 1 st at beg of next 2 rows—49 (51, 53, 55, 57, 57) sts. Work 2 rows even.

Next (dec) row: (RS) K1 (edge st), k2tog, work in est patt to last 3 sts, ssk, k1 (edge st)—2 sts dec'd.

Rep dec row every 4 rows 2 (2, 4, 5, 6, 8) more times, then every RS row 9 (10, 8, 8, 7, 5) times—25 (25, 27, 27, 29, 29) sts. Work 1 row even.

Next (double dec) row: (RS) K1 (edge st), k3tog, work in est patt to last 4 sts, sssk, k1 (edge st)—4 sts dec'd.

Rep double dec row once more—17 (17, 19, 19, 21, 21) sts. BO rem sts.

FINISHING

Weave in ends. Block pieces to finished measurements.

Sew shoulder seams.

Neckband

With crochet hook and RS facing, beg at left shoulder seam and work a rnd of sc along neck and placket edges, working 1 sc in each st and 1 sc in each row, skipping about every 4th row. Number of sc should be divisible by 4. Do not turn.

Next row: Ch 3, 4 tr in first sc, *skip 1 sc, 1 sl st in next sc, skip 1 sc, 5 tr in next sc; rep from * to last sc, skip next sc, 1 sl st in base of ch at beg of rnd. Fasten off.

Sew side and sleeve seams. Sew in sleeves.

Bottom edging

With crochet hook and RS facing, work 244 (260, 276, 296, 316, 340) sc along lower edge of body. Do not turn.

Next row: Ch 3, 4 tr in first sc, *skip 1 sc, 1 sl st in next sc, skip 1 sc, 5 tr in next sc; rep from * to last sc, skip next sc, 1 sl st in base of ch at beg of rnd. Fasten off.

Work edging around lower edge of each sleeve same as bottom.

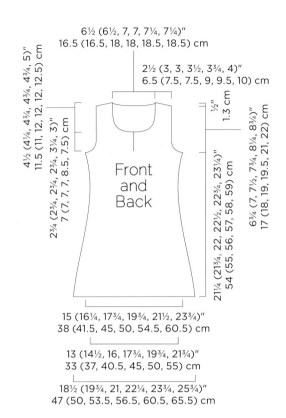

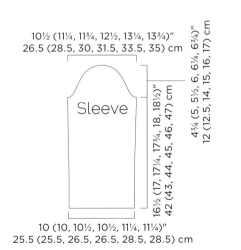

Short Sleeve Bolero

This is an easy-to-knit bolero with only one button. Combine it with the shoulder wrap/skirt on page 44, this time wearing the piece as a skirt. The instructions for the wrist warmers are in that same project.

Photo page 15

finished measurements

30½ (33½, 37, 40, 44½, 49½)" (77.5 [85, 94, 101.5, 113, 125.5] cm) bust circumference and 14¼ (15, 15¾, 16½, 17¼, 18)" (36 [38, 40, 42, 44, 46] cm) long. To fit woman's sizes x-small (small, medium, large, 1X, 2X). Shown in size medium.

yarn

Worsted weight (medium #4).

Marks & Kattens Eco Wool (100% eco-wool; 88 yd [80 m]/50 g): natural white 1979, 5 (5, 6, 6, 7, 7) balls.

needles

U.S. size 10 (6 mm) needles.

U.S. size 10½ (6.5 mm) needles.

Adjust needle sizes if necessary to obtain the correct gauge.

notions

Stitch holders; tapestry needle; one 1¼" (30 mm) button.

gauge

17 sts and 22 rows = 4" (10 cm) in rib patt on larger needles.

sts. Work new sts into patt. Continue even until piece measures 7 (7½, 7¾, 8¼, 8¾, 9)" (18 [19, 20, 21, 22, 23] cm), ending with a WS row.

Shape armholes

BO 4 (4, 5, 7, 10, 13) sts at beg of next 2 rows, 2 sts at beg of next 0 (2, 2, 2, 2, 4) rows, then 1 st at beg of next 4 (4, 6, 6, 6, 4) rows—53 (55, 57, 61, 65, 67) sts. Work even until armhole measures 6½ (6¾, 7¼, 7½, 7¾, 8¼)" (16.5 [17, 18.5, 19, 20, 21] cm), ending with a WS row.

Shape neck and shoulders

Next row: BO 8 (8, 8, 9, 10, 10) sts, work 8 (9, 9, 10, 10, 11) sts, place next 21 (21, 23, 23, 25, 25) sts onto holder for back neck, join a second ball of yarn and work to end of row. Continue each side separately.

Next row: BO 8 (8, 8, 9, 10, 10) sts, work to neck edge; on other side, BO 1 st, work to end.

Next row: BO 7 (8, 8, 9, 9, 10) sts; on other side, BO 1 st, work to end.

BO rem 7 (8, 8, 9, 9, 10) sts.

LEFT FRONT

With larger needles, CO 34 (38, 40, 44, 48, 52) sts.

Row 1: (WS) K1 (edge st), *p1, k1; rep from * to last st, k1 (edge st).

Row 2: K1 (edge st), *p1, k1; rep from * to last st, k1 (edge st).

Rep Rows 1 and 2 once more, then rep Row 1 once more.

Row 6: (RS) K1 (edge st), p3, *k1, p3; rep from * to last 6 (6, 8, 8, 8, 8) sts, k1, (p1, k1) 2 (2, 3, 3, 3, 3) times, k1 (edge st).

Row 7: K1 (edge st), (p1, k1) 2 (2, 3, 3, 3, 3) times, p1, *k3, p1; rep from * to last st, k1 (edge st).

Next (inc) row: (RS) K1 (edge st), M1, work in est patt to end of row—1 st inc'd.

Rep inc row every 8 (10, 8, 10, 8, 4) rows 3 (2, 4, 3, 4, 3) times, then every 6 rows 0 (0, 0, 0, 0, 4) times—38 (41, 45, 48, 53, 60)

BACK

With larger needles, CO 57 (65, 69, 77, 85, 89) sts.

Row 1: (WS) K1 (edge st), *k1, p1; rep from * to last 2 sts, k1, k1 (edge st).

Row 2: K1 (edge st), *p1, k1; rep from * to last 2 sts, p1, k1 (edge st).

Rep Rows 1 and 2 once more, then rep Row 1 once more.

Row 6: (RS) K1 (edge st), p3, *k1, p3*; rep from * to last st, k1 (edge st).

Row 7: K1 (edge st), k3, *p1, k3; rep from * to last st, k1 (edge st).

Next (inc) row: (RS), K1 (edge st), M1, work in patt to last st, M1, k1 (edge st)—2 sts inc'd.

Rep inc row every 8 (10, 8, 10, 8, 4) rows 3 (2, 4, 3, 4, 3) times, then every 6 rows 0 (0, 0, 0, 0, 4) times—65 (71, 79, 85, 95, 105)

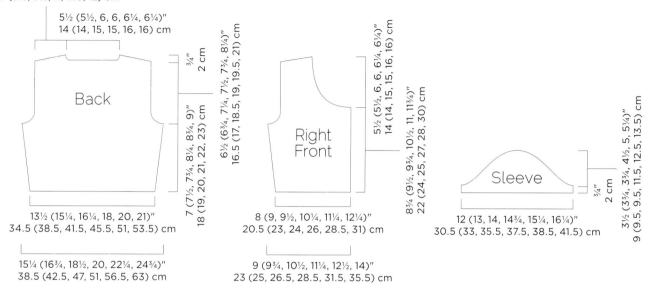

3½ (3¾, 3¾, 4¼, 4½, 4¾)"
9 (9.5, 9.5, 11, 11.5, 12) cm

5½ (5½, 6, 6, 6¼, 6¼)"
14 (14, 15, 15, 16, 16) cm

Back

¾"
2 cm

7 (7½, 7¾, 8¼, 8¾, 9)"
18 (19, 20, 21, 22, 23) cm

6½ (6¾, 7¼, 7½, 7¾, 8¼)"
16.5 (17, 18.5, 19, 19.5, 21) cm

13½ (15¼, 16¼, 18, 20, 21)"
34.5 (38.5, 41.5, 45.5, 51, 53.5) cm

15¼ (16¾, 18½, 20, 22¼, 24¾)"
38.5 (42.5, 47, 51, 56.5, 63) cm

Right
Front

5½ (5½, 6, 6, 6¼, 6¼)"
14 (14, 15, 15, 16, 16) cm

8¾ (9½, 9¾, 10½, 11, 11¾)"
22 (24, 25, 27, 28, 30) cm

8 (9, 9½, 10¼, 11¼, 12¼)"
20.5 (23, 24, 26, 28.5, 31) cm

9 (9¾, 10½, 11¼, 12½, 14)"
23 (25, 26.5, 28.5, 31.5, 35.5) cm

Sleeve

¾"
2 cm

3½ (3¾, 3¾, 4½, 5, 5¼)"
9 (9.5, 9.5, 11.5, 12.5, 13.5) cm

12 (13, 14, 14¾, 15¼, 16¼)"
30.5 (33, 35.5, 37.5, 38.5, 41.5) cm

sts. Work new sts into patt. Continue even until piece measures 7 (7½, 7¾, 8¼, 8¾, 9)" (18 [19, 20, 21, 22, 23] cm), ending with a WS row.

Shape armhole

BO at beg of RS rows 4 (4, 6, 7, 10, 13) sts once, 2 sts 0 (1, 1, 1, 1, 2) time(s), then 1 st 2 (2, 3, 3, 3, 2) times—32 (33, 34, 36, 38, 41) sts. Work even until piece measures 8¾ (9½, 9¾, 10½, 11, 11¾)" (22 [24, 25, 27, 28, 30] cm), ending with a WS row.

Shape neck

Next row: (RS) Work in patt to last 10 (10, 11, 11, 12, 14) sts, place rem sts onto holder for neck—22 (23, 23, 25, 26, 27) sts rem.

BO at beg of WS rows 3 sts once, 2 sts once, then 1 st twice—15 (16, 16, 18, 19, 20) sts rem. Work even until piece measures 6½ (6¾, 7¼, 7½, 7¾, 8¼)" (16.5 [17, 18.5, 19, 20, 21] cm), ending with a WS row.

Shape shoulder

BO at beg of RS rows 8 (8, 8, 9, 10, 10) sts once, then 7 (8, 8, 9, 9, 10) sts once.

RIGHT FRONT

With larger needles, CO 34 (38, 40, 44, 48, 52) sts.

Row 1: (WS) K1 (edge st), *k1, p1; rep from * to last st, k1 (edge st).

Row 2: K1 (edge st), *k1, p1; rep from * to last st, k1 (edge st).

Rep Rows 1 and 2 once more, then rep Row 1 once more.

Row 6: (RS) K1 (edge st), (k1, p1) 2 (2, 3, 3, 3, 3) times, *k1, p3; rep from * to last st, k1 (edge st).

Row 7: K1 (edge st), *k3, p1; rep from * to last 5 (5, 7, 7, 7, 7) sts, (k1, p1) 2 (2, 3, 3, 3, 3) times, k1 (edge st).

Next (inc) row: (RS) Work in est patt to last st, M1, k1 (edge st)—1 st inc'd.

Rep inc row every 8 (10, 8, 10, 8, 4) rows 3 (2, 4, 3, 4, 3) times, then every 6 rows 0 (0, 0, 0, 0, 4) times—38 (41, 45, 48, 53, 60) sts. Work new sts into patt. Continue even until piece measures 7 (7½, 7¾, 8¼, 8¾, 9)" (18 [19, 20, 21, 22, 23] cm), ending with a RS row.

Shape armhole

BO at beg of WS rows 4 (4, 6, 7, 10, 13) sts once, 2 sts 0 (1, 1, 1, 2) time(s), then 1 st 2 (2, 3, 3, 3, 2) times—32 (33, 34, 36, 38, 41) sts. Work even until piece measures 8¾ (9½, 9¾, 10½, 11, 11¾)" (22 [24, 25, 27, 28, 30] cm), ending with a RS row.

Shape neck

Next row: (WS) Work in patt to last 10 (10, 11, 11, 12, 14) sts, place rem sts onto holder for neck—22 (23, 23, 25, 26, 27) sts rem.

BO at beg of RS rows 3 sts once, 2 sts once, then 1 st twice—15 (16, 16, 18, 19, 20) sts rem. Work even until piece measures 6½ (6¾, 7¼, 7½, 7¾, 8¼)" (16.5 [17, 18.5, 19, 20, 21] cm), ending with a RS row.

Shape shoulder

BO at beg of WS rows 8 (8, 8, 9, 10, 10) sts once, then 7 (8, 8, 9, 9, 10) sts once.

SLEEVES

With smaller needles, CO 51 (55, 59, 63, 65, 69) sts.

Row 1: (WS) K1 (edge st), *k1, p1; rep from * to last 2 sts, k1, k1 (edge st).

Row 2: K1 (edge st), *p1, k1; rep from * to last 2 sts, p1, k1 (edge st).

Rep Row 1 once more.

Row 4: (RS) K1 (edge st), p2 (2, 2, 2, 3, 3), k1, *p3, k1; rep from * to last 3 (3, 3, 3, 4, 4) sts, p2 (2, 2, 2, 3, 3), k1 (edge st).

Row 5: K1 (edge st), k2 (2, 2, 2, 3, 3), *p1, k3; rep from * to last 4 (4, 4, 4, 5, 5) sts, p1, k2 (2, 2, 2, 3, 3), k1 (edge st).

Shape cap

BO 5 (5, 6, 7, 7, 8) sts at beg of next 2 rows, then 1 st at the beg of next 2 rows—39 (43, 45, 47, 49, 51) sts.

Next (dec) row: (RS) K1 (edge st), k2tog, work in est patt to last 3 sts, ssk, k1 (edge st)—2 sts dec'd.

Rep dec row every RS row 5 (5, 6, 8, 10, 11) more times. Work 1 WS row even.

Next (double dec) row: (RS) K1 (edge st), k3tog, work in est patt to last 4 sts, sssk, k1 (edge st)—4 sts dec'd.

Rep double dec row every RS row 1 (2, 1, 1, 0, 0) more time(s)—19 (19, 21, 21, 23, 23) sts.

BO rem sts.

FINISHING

Weave in ends. Block pieces to finished measurements. Seam shoulders.

Neckband

With smaller needles and RS facing, [k1 (edge st), (k1, p1) 4 (4, 5, 5, 5, 6) times, k1 (1, 0, 0, 1, 1)] over held 10 (10, 11, 11, 12, 14) sts at right neck, pick up and k27 sts along right front neck to shoulder, 2 sts along right back neck, [k1 (1, 0, 0, 1, 1), (p1, k1) 10 (10, 11, 11, 12, 12) times from held 21 (21, 23, 23, 25, 25) sts at back neck, pick up and k2 sts along left back neck, 27 sts along left front neck, [k1 (1, 0, 0, 1, 1), (p1, k1) 4 (4, 5, 5, 5, 6) times, k1 (edge st)] from held 10 (10, 11, 11, 12, 14) sts at left neck—99 (99, 103, 103, 107, 111) sts.

Next row: (WS) K1 (edge st), *p1, k1; rep from * to last 2 sts, p1, k1 (edge st).

Work 2 more rows of rib as est.

Next (buttonhole) row: (RS) K1 (edge st), k1, p1, k0 (0, 1, 1, 1, 1), BO 3 in rib, work to end of row.

Next row: CO 3 sts over buttonhole gap.

Work 2 more rows of rib.

BO loosely in rib.

Sew side and sleeve seams. Sew in sleeves. Sew button to left neckband under buttonhole.

Texture Knit Cardigan

This cardigan has a lovely block pattern and a collar that requires a bit of concentration to work. It's the perfect jacket for cool summer evenings or to wear as an extra layer in the winter.

Photos pages 16 and 17

finished measurements

31 (33¾, 36¾, 39¾, 43¼, 47¾)" (78.5 [85.5, 93.5, 101, 110, 121.5] cm) bust circumference and 22¼ (22¾, 23¾, 24½, 25¼, 26¼)" (56.5 [58, 60.5, 62, 64, 66.5] cm) long. To fit woman's sizes x-small (small, medium, large, 1X, 2X). Shown in size medium.

yarn

Baby weight (fine #2).

Marks & Kattens Eco Baby Wool (100% eco-wool; 91 yd [83 m]/25 g): natural white 173, 14 (16, 17, 19, 20, 22) balls.

needles

U.S. size 6 (4 mm) needles.

Adjust needle sizes if necessary to obtain the correct gauge.

notions

Five locking markers or safety pins; stitch holders; tapestry needle; five ¾" (19 mm) buttons.

gauge

22 sts and 36 rows = 4" (10 cm) in texture patt.

BACK

CO 87 (95, 103, 111, 121, 133) sts. Knit 1 WS row.

Next row: (RS) K1 (edge st), beg at your size on right side of Texture Patt back chart and work 5 (9, 3, 7, 2, 8) sts, rep next 10 sts 7 (8, 9, 10, 11, 12) times, work rem 10 (4, 8, 2, 7, 3) sts of chart, k1 (edge st).

Next row: K1 (edge st), beg at your size on left side of Texture Patt back chart and work 10 (4, 8, 2, 7, 3) sts, rep next 10 sts 7 (8, 9, 10, 11, 12) times, work rem 5 (9, 3, 7, 2, 8) sts of chart, k1 (edge st).

Continue patt as est until piece measures ¾" (2 cm) from beg, ending with a WS row.

Next (dec) row: (RS) K2 (edge st), ssk, work in patt to last 3 sts, k2tog, k1 (edge st)—2 sts dec'd.

Rep dec row every 6 rows 4 (5, 5, 10, 10, 11) times, then every 4 rows 5 (4, 5, 0, 0, 0) times—67 (75, 81, 89, 99, 109) sts. Work even until piece measures 6¾ (7, 7½, 8¼, 8¾, 9)" (17 [18, 19, 21, 22, 23] cm) from beg, ending with a WS row.

Next (inc) row: (RS) K1 (edge st), M1, work in est patt to last st, M1, k1 (edge st)—2 sts inc'd.

Rep inc row every 6 rows 9 (4, 5, 8, 10, 11) times, then every 8 rows 0 (5, 5, 2, 0, 0) times—87 (95, 103, 111, 121, 133) sts. Work even until piece measures 15 (15¼, 15¾, 16¼, 16½, 17)" (38 [39, 40, 41, 42, 43] cm) from beg, ending with a WS row.

Shape armhole

BO 7 (8, 10, 10, 13, 15) sts at beg of next 2 rows, 3 sts at beg of next 0 (0, 0, 0, 0, 2) rows, 2 sts at beg of next 2 (2, 2, 4, 4, 2) rows, then 1 st at beg of next 4 (4, 4, 4, 4, 6) rows—65 (71, 75, 79, 83, 87) sts rem. Work even until armhole measures 6¾ (7, 7½, 7¾, 8¼, 8¾)" (17 [18, 19, 20, 21, 22] cm), ending with a WS row.

Shape neck and shoulders

Next row: (RS) BO 7 (8, 8, 9, 9, 10) sts, work 14 (16, 17, 18, 19, 20) sts, place center 23 (23, 25, 25, 27, 27) sts onto holder for neck, join a second ball of yarn, work to end. Work each side separately.

Next row: BO 7 (8, 8, 9, 9, 10) sts, work to 2 sts before next edge, p2tog; on other side, BO 1 st, work to end.

Next row: BO 6 (7, 8, 8, 9, 9) sts, work to 2 sts before neck edge, k2tog; on other side, BO 1 st, work to end.

Next row: BO 6 (7, 8, 9, 9) sts, work to neck edge; on other side, work to end.

BO 6 (7, 7, 8, 8, 9) sts at beg of next 2 rows.

LEFT FRONT

CO 48 (52, 56, 60, 65, 71) sts. Knit 1 WS row.

Next row: (RS) K1 (edge st), beg at your size on right side of Texture Patt left front chart and work 5 (9, 3, 7, 2, 8) sts, rep next 10 sts 3 (3, 4, 4, 5, 5) times, work rem 4 sts of chart, k8 (buttonband).

Next row: K8 (buttonband), beg at left side of Texture Patt left front chart and work 4 sts, rep next 10 sts 3 (3, 4, 4, 5, 5) times, work rem 5 (9, 3, 7, 2, 8) sts of chart, k1 (edge st).

Texture Pattern, back

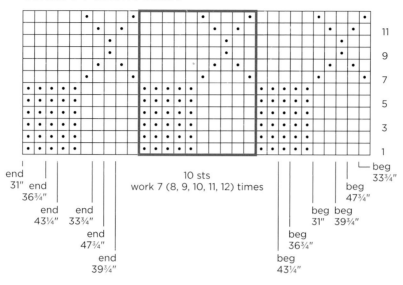

end
31" end
36¾"

end   end
43¼"   33¾"

end
47¾"

end
39¾"

10 sts
work 7 (8, 9, 10, 11, 12) times

beg
33¾"

beg
47¾"

beg   beg
31"   39¾"

beg
36¾"

beg
43¼"

Texture Pattern, left front

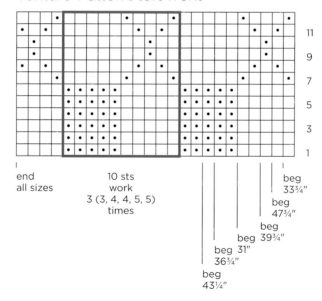

☐ k on RS; p on WS

• p on RS; k on WS

☐ pattern repeat

end
all sizes

10 sts
work
3 (3, 4, 4, 5, 5)
times

beg
33¾"

beg
47¾"

beg
beg 39¾"

beg 31"
36¾"

beg
43¼"

Continue patt as est until piece measures ¾" (2 cm) from beg, ending with a WS row.

Next (dec) row: (RS) K1 (edge st), ssk, work as est to end—1 st dec'd.

Rep dec row every 6 rows 4 (5, 5, 10, 10, 11) times, then every 4 rows 5 (4, 5, 0, 0, 0) times—38 (42, 45, 49, 54, 59) sts. Work even until piece measures 6¾ (7, 7½, 8¼, 8¾, 9)" (17 [18, 19, 21, 22, 23] cm) from beg, ending with a WS row.

Next (inc) row: (RS) K1 (edge st), M1, work as est to end—1 st inc'd.

Rep inc row every 6 rows 9 (4, 5, 8, 10, 11) times, then every 8 rows 0 (5, 5, 2, 0, 0) times—48 (52, 56, 60, 65, 71) sts.

Note: Read through rem instructions for left front as shaping for armhole, lapel, neck, and shoulders all take place simultaneously.

Work even until piece measures 14½ (15¼, 15¾, 16½, 17, 17¾)" (37 [39, 40, 42, 43, 45] cm), shape lapel every 4 rows 9 times on a RS row as foll: work to last st, M1, k1. AT THE SAME TIME, work 1 more st in garter st on first WS row after first inc, then every 4 rows 10 (10, 11, 11, 12, 12) times more; width of lapel increases 1 st each time and number of sts in Texture Patt dec by 1 st each time. AT THE SAME TIME, when piece measures 15 (15¼, 15¾, 16¼, 16½, 17)" (38 [39, 40, 41, 42, 43] cm), shape armhole as foll: BO at beg of RS rows 7 (8, 10, 10, 13, 15) sts once, 3 sts 0 (0, 0, 0, 0, 1) time, 2 sts 1 (1, 1, 2, 2, 1) time(s), then 1 st 2 (2, 2, 2, 2, 3) times—46 (49, 51, 53, 55, 57) sts rem when lapel and collar shaping are complete.

When piece measures about 19¼ (19¾, 20¾, 21¾, 22¼, 23¼)" (49 [50, 52.5, 55, 56.5, 59] cm) from beg, end with a RS row.

Shape neck

BO 27 (27, 28, 28, 29, 29) sts at beg of next row—19 (22, 23, 25, 26, 28) sts rem.

Work even until armhole measures 6¾ (7, 7½, 7¾, 8¼, 8¾)" (17 [18, 19, 21, 22, 23] cm), ending with a WS row and same patt row as for back.

Shape shoulder

BO at beg of RS rows 10 sts 0 (0, 0, 0, 0, 1) time, 9 sts 0 (0, 0, 1, 2, 2) time(s), 8 sts 0 (1, 2, 2, 1, 0) time(s), 7 sts 1 (2, 1, 0, 0, 0) time(s), then 6 sts 2 (0, 0, 0, 0, 0) times.

Place markers (pm) along buttonband for buttons, placing bottom m at 6th row above bottom edge, top m ¾" (2 cm) below first lapel inc, then evenly space rem m in between.

RIGHT FRONT

CO 48 (52, 56, 60, 65, 71) sts. Knit 1 WS row.

Next row: (RS) K8 (buttonhole band), beg at right side of Texture Patt right front chart and work 9 sts, rep next 10 sts 2 (3, 3, 4, 4, 5) times, work rem 10 (4, 8, 2, 7, 3) sts of chart, k1 (edge st).

Next row: K1 (edge st), beg at your size on left side of Texture Patt left front chart and work 10 (4, 8, 2, 7, 3) sts, rep next 10 sts 2 (3, 3, 4, 4, 5) times, work rem 9 sts of chart, k8 (buttonhole band).

Continue patt as est until piece measures ¾" (2 cm) from beg, ending with a WS row.

Next (dec) row: (RS) Work as est to last 3 sts, k2tog, k1 (edge st)—1 st dec'd.

Rep dec row every 6 rows 4 (5, 5, 10, 10, 11) times, then every 4 rows 5 (4, 5, 0, 0, 0) times—38 (42, 45, 49, 54, 59) sts. AT THE SAME TIME, at beg of 6th row, make buttonhole on next RS row as foll: K3, BO 2 sts for buttonhole, work to end. On next row, CO 2 sts over buttonhole gap. Work 4 more buttonholes to match m on buttonband. AT THE SAME TIME, when piece measures 6¾ (7, 7½, 8¼, 8¾, 9)" (17 [18, 19, 21, 22, 23] cm) from beg, end with a WS row.

Next (inc) row: (RS) Work as est to last st, M1, k1 (edge st)—1 st inc'd.

Rep inc row every 6 rows 9 (4, 5, 8, 10, 11) times, then every 8 rows 0 (5, 5, 2, 0, 0) times—48 (52, 56, 60, 65, 71) sts.

Note: Read through rem instructions for left front as shaping for armhole, lapel, neck, and shoulders all take place simultaneously.

Texture Pattern, right front

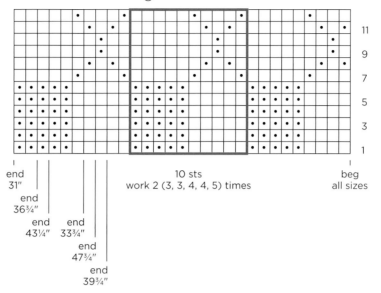

end
31"

end
36¾"

end
43¼"

end
33¾"

end
47¾"

end
39¾"

10 sts
work 2 (3, 3, 4, 4, 5) times

beg
all sizes

	k on RS; p on WS
·	p on RS; k on WS
	pattern repeat

Texture Pattern, sleeve

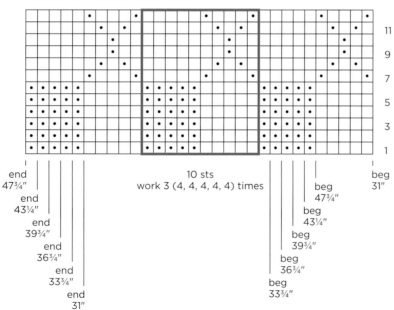

end
47¾"

end
43¼"

end
39¾"

end
36¾"

end
33¾"

end
31"

10 sts
work 3 (4, 4, 4, 4, 4) times

beg
47¾"

beg
43¼"

beg
39¾"

beg
36¾"

beg
33¾"

beg
31"

Work even until piece measures 14½ (15¼, 15¾, 16½, 17, 17¾)" (37 [39, 40, 42, 43, 45] cm), shape lapel every 4 rows 9 times on a RS row as foll: K1, M1, work to end. AT THE SAME TIME, work 1 more st in garter st on first WS row after first inc, then every 4 rows 10 (10, 11, 11, 12, 12) times more; width of lapel increases 1 st each time and number of sts in Texture Patt dec by 1 st each time. AT THE SAME TIME, when piece measures 15 (15¼, 15¾, 16¼, 16½, 17)" (38 [39, 40, 41, 42, 43] cm), shape armhole as foll: BO at beg of WS rows 7 (8, 10, 10, 13, 15) sts once, 3 sts 0 (0, 0, 0, 0, 1) time, 2 sts 1 (1, 1, 2, 2, 1) time(s), then 1 st 2 (2, 2, 2, 2, 3) times—46 (49, 51, 53, 55, 57) sts rem when lapel and collar shaping are complete.

When piece measures about 19¼ (19¾, 20¾, 21¾, 22¼, 23¼)" (49 [50, 52.5, 55, 56.5, 59] cm) from beg, end with a WS row.

Shape neck

BO 27 (27, 28, 28, 29, 29) at beg of next row—19 (22, 23, 25, 26, 28) sts rem.

Work even until armhole measures 6¾ (7, 7½, 8¼, 8¾, 9)" (17 [18, 19, 21, 22, 23] cm), ending with a RS row and same patt row as for back.

Shape shoulder

BO at beg of WS rows 10 sts 0 (0, 0, 0, 0, 1) time, 9 sts 0 (0, 1, 2, 2) time(s), 8 sts 0 (1, 2, 2, 1, 0) time(s), 7 sts 1 (2, 1, 0, 0, 0) time(s), then 6 sts 2 (0, 0, 0, 0, 0) times.

SLEEVES

CO 47 (49, 51, 53, 55, 57) sts. Knit 1 WS row.

Next row: (RS) K1 (edge st), beg at your size on right side of Texture Patt sleeve chart, work 10 (1, 2, 3, 4, 5) st(s), work next 10 sts 3 (4, 4, 4, 4, 4) times, work rem 5 (6, 7, 8, 9, 10) sts of chart, k1 (edge st).

Next row: K1 (edge st), beg at your size on left side of Texture Patt sleeve chart, work 5 (6, 7, 8, 9, 10) sts, work next 10 sts 3 (4, 4, 4, 4, 4) times, work rem 10 (1, 2, 3, 4, 5) st(s), k1 (edge st).

Continue patt as est until piece measures 2¼" (6 cm), ending with a WS row.

Next (inc) row: (RS) K1 (edge st), M1, work in est patt to last st, M1, k1 (edge st)—2 sts inc'd.

Rep inc row every 6 rows 0 (0, 10, 15, 19, 25) times, then every 8 rows 15 (17, 9, 6, 4, 0) times—63 (67, 71, 75, 79, 83) sts. Work new sts in patt.

Work even until piece measures 17¼ (17¾, 18, 18½, 19, 19¼)" (44 [45, 46, 47, 48, 49] cm) from beg, ending with a WS row.

Shape cap

BO 6 (7, 8, 9, 10, 12) sts at beg of next 2 rows, then 1 st at beg of next 2 rows—49 (51, 53, 55, 57, 57) sts rem.

Work 2 rows even.

Next (dec) row: (RS) K1 (edge st), k2tog, work in patt as est to last 3 sts, ssk, k1 (edge st)—2 sts dec'd.

Rep dec row every 4 rows 2 (4, 5, 6, 8) times, then every row 9 (10, 8, 8, 7, 5) times—25 (25, 27, 27, 29, 29) sts. Work 1 WS row even.

Next (double dec) row: (RS) K1 (edge st), k3tog, work to last 4 sts, sssk, k1 (edge st)—4 sts dec'd.

Rep double dec row every RS row once more.

BO rem 17 (17, 19, 19, 21, 21) sts.

FINISHING

Weave in ends. Block pieces to finished measurements.

Sew shoulder seams.

Collar

With WS facing, beg at left front neck, pick up and k22 (24, 25, 27, 28, 30) sts along left neck, k23 (23, 25, 25, 27, 27) sts from holder at back neck, then pick up and k22 (24, 25, 27, 28, 30) sts along right neck edge; do not pick up sts along bound-off lapel sts—67 (71, 75, 79, 83, 87) sts. Knit 1 row.

Next (inc) row: (RS of collar) K1, M1, knit to last st, M1, k1— 2 sts inc'd.

Rep inc row every RS row of collar 7 (8, 8, 9, 9) more times. AT THE SAME TIME, when collar measures about ¾" (2 cm), inc

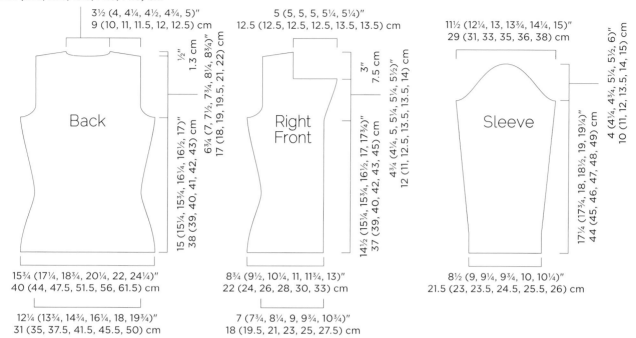

Back

5 (5, 5¼, 5¼, 5¾, 5¾)"
12.5 (12.5, 13.5, 13.5, 14.5, 14.5) cm

3½ (4, 4¼, 4½, 4¾, 5)"
9 (10, 11, 11.5, 12, 12.5) cm

½"
1.3 cm

6¾ (7, 7½, 7¾, 8¼, 8¾)"
17 (18, 19, 19.5, 21, 22) cm

15 (15¼, 15¾, 16¼, 16½, 17)"
38 (39, 40, 41, 42, 43) cm

15¾ (17¼, 18¾, 20¼, 22, 24¼)"
40 (44, 47.5, 51.5, 56, 61.5) cm

12¼ (13¾, 14¾, 16¼, 18, 19¾)"
31 (35, 37.5, 41.5, 45.5, 50) cm

Right Front

5 (5, 5, 5, 5¼, 5¼)"
12.5 (12.5, 12.5, 12.5, 13.5, 13.5) cm

3"
7.5 cm

4¾ (4¼, 5, 5¼, 5¼, 5½)"
12 (11, 12.5, 13.5, 13.5, 14) cm

14½ (15¼, 15¾, 16½, 17, 17¾)"
37 (39, 40, 42, 43, 45) cm

8¾ (9½, 10¼, 11, 11¾, 13)"
22 (24, 26, 28, 30, 33) cm

7 (7¾, 8¼, 9, 9¾, 10¾)"
18 (19.5, 21, 23, 25, 27.5) cm

Sleeve

11½ (12¼, 13, 13¾, 14¼, 15)"
29 (31, 33, 35, 36, 38) cm

4 (4¼, 4¾, 5¼, 5½, 6)"
10 (11, 12, 13.5, 14, 15) cm

17¼ (17¾, 18, 18½, 19, 19¼)"
44 (45, 46, 47, 48, 49) cm

8½ (9, 9¼, 9¾, 10, 10¼)"
21.5 (23, 23.5, 24.5, 25.5, 26) cm

10 sts evenly spaced over the center 41 sts—93 (97, 103, 107, 113, 117) sts.

Work 21 (21, 23, 23, 25, 25) rows even. BO all sts loosely.

Sew inc edges of collar to bound-off edge of lapel; seam should be about 2 (2, 2¼, 2¼, 2½, 2½)" (5 [5, 5.5, 5.5, 6.5, 6.5] cm) long.

Sew side and sleeve seams. Sew in sleeves. Sew buttons to buttonband.

Texture Knit Vest

This vest is worked in the same block pattern as the cardigan, but it's easier to knit because there are no sleeves or collar. Wear it over a blouse or alone as a top.

Photos pages 16 and 17

finished measurements

29½ (32¼, 35¼, 38¼, 41¾, 46¼)" (75 [82, 89.5, 97, 106, 117.5] cm) bust circumference and 22¼ (22¾, 23¾, 24¾, 25¼, 26¼)" (56.5 [58, 60.5, 63, 64, 66.5] cm) long. To fit woman's sizes x-small (small, medium, large, 1X, 2X). Shown in size medium.

yarn

Baby weight (fine #2).

Marks & Kattens Eco Baby Wool (100% eco-wool; 91 yd [83 m]/25 g): natural white 173, 7 (8, 8, 9, 10, 11) balls.

needles

U.S. sizes 2.5 (3 mm) needles.

U.S. size 6 (4.5 mm) needles.

Adjust needle sizes if necessary to obtain the correct gauge.

notions

Removable stitch marker or safety pin; stitch holders; tapestry needle.

gauge

22 sts and 36 rows = 4" (10 cm) in Texture Patt on larger needles.

BACK

With larger needles, CO 83 (91, 99, 107, 117, 129) sts. Knit 1 WS row.

Next row: (RS) K1 (edge st), beg at your size on right side of Texture Patt chart and work 3 (7, 1, 5, 10, 6) st(s), rep next 10 sts 7 (8, 9, 9, 9, 12) times, work rem 9 (2, 6, 10, 5, 1) st(s) of chart, k1 (edge st).

Next row: K1 (edge st), beg at your size on left side of Texture Patt chart and work 9 (2, 6, 10, 5, 1) st(s), rep next 10 sts 7 (8, 9, 9, 9, 12) times, work rem 3 (7, 1, 5, 10, 6) st(s), k1 (edge st).

Continue patt as est until piece measures ¾" (2 cm) from beg, ending with a WS row.

Next (dec) row: (RS) K1 (edge st), ssk, work in patt to last 3 sts, k2tog, k1 (edge st)—2 sts dec'd.

Rep dec row every 6 rows 5 (5, 6, 10, 10, 11) times, then every 4 rows 4 (4, 4, 0, 0, 0) times—63 (71, 77, 85, 95, 105) sts. Work even until piece measures 6¾ (7, 7½, 8¼, 8¾, 9)" (17 [18, 19, 21, 22, 23] cm) from beg, ending with a WS row.

Next (inc) row: (RS) K1, (edge st), M1, work in est patt to last st, M1, k1 (edge st)—2 sts inc'd.

Rep inc row every 6 rows 3 (3, 6, 8, 10, 11) times, then every 8 rows 6 (6, 4, 2, 0, 0) times—83 (91, 99, 107, 117, 129) sts. Work even until piece measures 15 (15¼, 15¾, 16¼, 16½, 17)" (38 [39, 40, 41, 42, 43] cm), from beg, ending with a WS row.

Shape armhole

BO 9 (10, 12, 12, 14, 17) sts at beg of next 2 rows, 3 sts at beg of next 0 (0, 0, 0, 0, 2) rows, 2 sts at beg of next 2 (2, 2, 4, 4, 2) rows, then 1 st at beg of next 4 (4, 4, 4, 6, 6) rows—57 (63, 67, 71, 75, 79) sts rem. Work even until armhole measures 6¾ (7, 7½, 7¾, 8¼, 8¾)" (17 [18, 19, 19.5, 21, 22] cm), ending with a WS row.

Shape neck and shoulders

Next row: (RS) BO 6 (7, 7, 8, 8, 9) sts, work 12 (14, 15, 16, 17, 18) sts, place center 21 (21, 23, 23, 25, 25) sts onto holder for neck, join a second ball of yarn, work to end. Work each side separately.

Next row: BO 6 (7, 7, 8, 8, 9) sts, work to 2 sts before neck edge, p2tog; on other side, BO 1 st, work to end.

Next row: BO 5 (6, 7, 7, 8, 8) sts, work to 2 sts before neck edge, k2tog; on other side, BO 1 st, work to end.

Next row: BO 5 (6, 7, 7, 8, 8) sts, work to neck edge; on other side, work to end.

BO 5 (6, 6, 7, 7, 8) sts at beg of next 2 rows.

FRONT

Work front as for back until piece measures 15 (15¼, 15¾, 16¼, 16½, 17)" (38 [39, 40, 41, 42, 43] cm), from beg, ending with a WS row. Place marker (pm) onto center st.

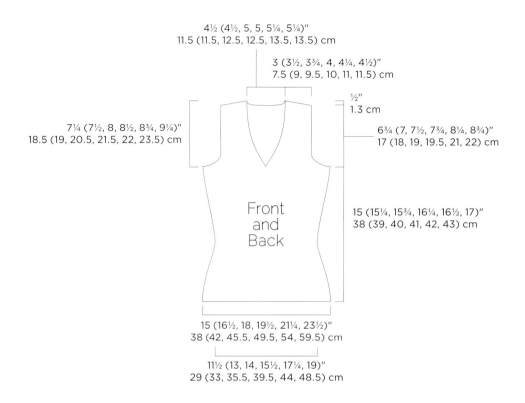

4½ (4½, 5, 5, 5¼, 5¼)"
11.5 (11.5, 12.5, 12.5, 13.5, 13.5) cm

3 (3½, 3¾, 4, 4¼, 4½)"
7.5 (9, 9.5, 10, 11, 11.5) cm

½"
1.3 cm

7¼ (7½, 8, 8½, 8¾, 9¼)"
18.5 (19, 20.5, 21.5, 22, 23.5) cm

6¾ (7, 7½, 7¾, 8¼, 8¾)"
17 (18, 19, 19.5, 21, 22) cm

Front
and
Back

15 (15¼, 15¾, 16¼, 16½, 17)"
38 (39, 40, 41, 42, 43) cm

15 (16½, 18, 19½, 21¼, 23½)"
38 (42, 45.5, 49.5, 54, 59.5) cm

11½ (13, 14, 15½, 17¼, 19)"
29 (33, 35.5, 39.5, 44, 48.5) cm

Shape armholes and neck

Next row: (RS) BO 9 (10, 12, 12, 14, 17) sts, work to marked st, place center st onto holder, join a second ball of yarn and work to end. Work each side separately.

Next row: BO 9 (10, 12, 12, 14, 17) sts, work to neck, CO 1 st (edge st); other side, CO 1 st (edge sts), work to end.

BO 3 sts at beg of next 0 (0, 0, 0, 0, 2) rows, 2 sts at beg of next 2 (2, 2, 4, 4, 2) rows, then 1 st at beg of next 4 (4, 4, 4, 6, 6) rows and AT THE SAME TIME, dec at neck edge every RS row 9 (9, 9, 9, 7, 7) times, then every 4 rows 4 (4, 5, 5, 7, 8) times—16 (19, 20, 22, 23, 25) sts rem. Work even until armhole measures 6¾ (7, 7½, 7¾, 8¼, 8¾)" (17 [18, 19, 19.5, 21, 22] cm), ending with a WS row, and same patt row as for back.

Shape shoulders

BO 9 sts at beg of next 0 (0, 0, 0, 0, 2) rows, 8 sts at beg of next 0 (0, 0, 2, 4, 4) rows, 7 sts at beg of next 0 (2, 4, 4, 2, 0) rows, 6 sts at beg of next 2 (4, 2, 0, 0, 0) rows, then 5 sts at beg of next 4 (0, 0, 0, 0, 0) rows.

FINISHING

Weave in ends. Block pieces to finished measurements.

Sew right shoulder seam.

Neckband

With smaller needles and RS facing, beg at left front shoulder, pick up and knit 52 (54, 58, 60, 62, 66) sts along left front neck, knit center st from holder, pick up and knit 57 (59, 63, 65,

Texture Pattern

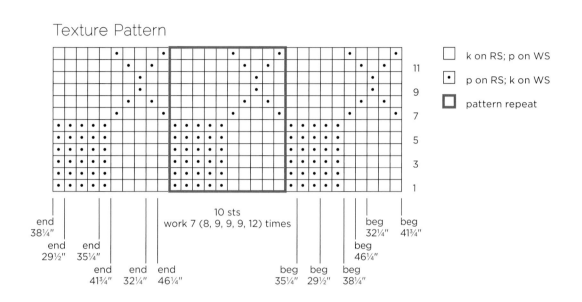

k on RS; p on WS

p on RS; k on WS

pattern repeat

10 sts
work 7 (8, 9, 9, 12) times

end
38¼"

end
29½"

end
35¼"

end
41¾"

end
32¼"

end
46¼"

beg
35¼"

beg
29½"

beg
38¼"

beg
32¼"

beg
46¼"

beg
41¾"

67, 71) sts along right neck, knit 21 (21, 23, 23, 25, 25) sts from holder at back neck, then pick up and knit 5 sts along left back neck—136 (140, 150, 154, 160, 168) sts.

Row 1: (WS) *P1, k1; rep from * to end.

Row 2: (K1, p1) to 2 sts before center st of front, p2tog, k1, ssp, (p1, k1) to last st, k1—2 sts dec'd.

Row 3: (P1, k1) to 2 sts before center st, p2, k1, p2, (k1, p1) to end.

Row 4: (K1, p1) to 3 sts before center st, k1, p2tog, k1, ssp, (k1, p1) to end—2 sts dec'd.

Row 5: Rep Row 1.

BO loosely in rib and dec as for Row 2 at center st.

Armhole edgings

With smaller needles and RS facing, pick up and knit 1 st in each st along lower section of armhole, then 4 sts for every 5 rows along sides of armhole. Work in k1, p1 rib for 5 rows. BO loosely in rib.

Sew left shoulder and neckband seam. Sew side seams.

Stockinette Dress with Garter Stitch Edgings and Flower

Here's a smart dress embellished with a decorative knit flower. The lower edge of the dress and the neckband are bordered with garter stitch. The bell shape makes a pleasingly full skirt.

Photos pages 18 and 19

finished measurements

32 (34, 38¼, 41¼, 45½, 49½)" (81.5 [86.5, 97, 105, 115.5, 125.5] cm) bust circumference and 32 (33, 33½, 34½, 35¼, 36)" (81.5 [84, 85, 87.5, 89.5, 91.5] cm) long. To fit woman's sizes x-small (small, medium, large, 1X, 2X). Shown in size medium.

yarn

Worsted weight (medium #4).

Marks & Kattens Eco Wool (100% eco-wool; 88 yd [80 m]/50 g): natural white 1979, 11 (11, 12, 13, 14, 15) balls.

needles

U.S. size 10 (6 mm) needles.

U.S. size 10½ (6.5 mm) needles.

Adjust needle sizes if necessary to obtain the correct gauge.

notions

Stitch markers (m); stitch holders; tapestry needle; one 1¼" (32 mm) button for flower.

gauge

15½ sts and 22 rows = 4" (10 cm) in St st on larger needles.

Note

Stitch markers are used to indicate placement for decreases used to shape the skirt; slip markers as you come to them.

BACK

With larger needles, CO 110 (114, 126, 132, 144, 152) sts. Beg on WS, work in garter st (knit every row) for 1" (2.5 cm), ending with a WS row.

Next (dec) row: (RS) K1 (edge st), ssk, k18 (20, 22, 24, 26, 29), place marker (pm), ssk, k20 (20, 22, 22, 24, 24), ssk, pm, k20 (20, 24, 26, 30, 32), pm, k2tog, k20 (20, 22, 22, 24, 24), k2tog, pm, k18 (20, 22, 24, 26, 29), k2tog, k1 (edge st)—6 sts dec'd.

Knit 9 rows even.

Next (dec) row: (RS) K1 (edge st), ssk, k17 (19, 21, 23, 25, 28), ssk, k18 (18, 20, 20, 22, 22), ssk, k20 (20, 24, 26, 30, 32), k2tog, k18 (18, 20, 20, 22, 22), k2tog, k17 (19, 21, 23, 25, 28), k2tog, k1 (edge st)—6 sts dec'd.

Rep dec row every 10 rows 4 times more, then every 8 rows 5 (5, 6, 6, 7, 7) more times, with 1 fewer st before first and after last m, 2 fewer sts between first and 2nd m, and 3rd and 4th m, and same number of sts between 2nd and 3rd m. AT THE SAME TIME, when piece measures 5½" (14 cm) from beg, change to St st on next RS row as foll:

Next row: (RS) Knit.

Next row: K1 (edge st), purl to last st, k1 (edge st). When all dec are complete, 50 (54, 60, 66, 72, 80) sts rem. Remove m on last dec row. Work even until piece measures 17 (17¼, 17¾, 18½, 19, 19¼)" (43 [44, 45, 47, 48, 49] cm) from beg, ending with a WS row.

Next (inc) row: (RS) K1 (edge st), M1, knit to last st, M1, k1 (edge st)—2 sts inc'd.

Rep inc row every 4 rows 0 (3, 3, 3, 5, 5) times, then every 6 rows 6 (4, 4, 4, 3, 3) times—64 (70, 76, 82, 90, 98) sts. Work even until piece measures 24¾ (25¼, 25½, 26, 26½, 26¾)" (63 [64, 65, 66, 67, 68] cm) from beg, ending with a WS row.

Shape armholes

BO 3 (4, 4, 6, 9, 11) sts at beg of next 2 rows—58 (62, 68, 70, 72, 76) sts.

Next (dec) row: (RS) K1, k2tog, knit to last 3 sts, ssk, k1 (edge st)—2 sts dec'd.

Rep dec row every RS row 0 (1, 2, 2, 2, 2) more time(s)—56 (58, 62, 64, 66, 70) sts rem. Work even until armhole measures 6¼ (6¾, 7, 7½, 7¾, 8¼)" (16 [17, 18, 19, 20, 21] cm), ending with a WS row.

Shape shoulders and neck

Next row: (RS) BO 5 (5, 6, 6, 6, 7) sts, work 17 (17, 18, 19, 19, 21) sts, place center 22 (24, 26, 26, 28, 28) sts onto holder for neck, join a second ball of yarn, work to end. Work each side separately.

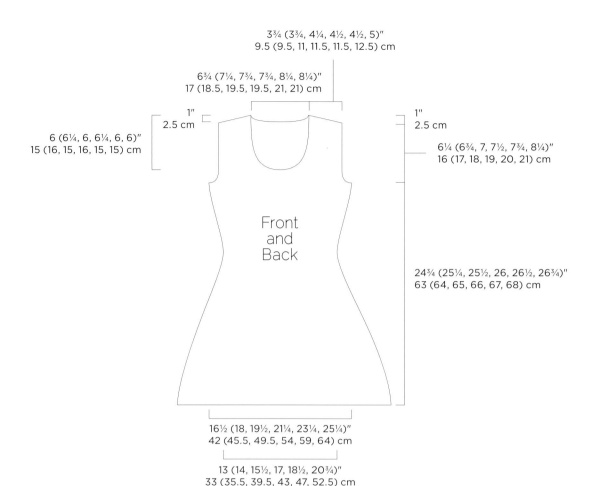

3¾ (3¾, 4¼, 4½, 4½, 5)"
9.5 (9.5, 11, 11.5, 11.5, 12.5) cm

6¾ (7¼, 7¾, 7¾, 8¼, 8¼)"
17 (18.5, 19.5, 19.5, 21, 21) cm

1"
2.5 cm

1"
2.5 cm

6 (6¼, 6, 6¼, 6, 6)"
15 (16, 15, 16, 15, 15) cm

6¼ (6¾, 7, 7½, 7¾, 8¼)"
16 (17, 18, 19, 20, 21) cm

Front
and
Back

24¾ (25¼, 25½, 26, 26½, 26¾)"
63 (64, 65, 66, 67, 68) cm

16½ (18, 19½, 21¼, 23¼, 25¼)"
42 (45.5, 49.5, 54, 59, 64) cm

13 (14, 15½, 17, 18½, 20¾)"
33 (35.5, 39.5, 43, 47, 52.5) cm

29¼ (30½, 33½, 35¼, 38½, 40½)"
74.5 (77.5, 85, 89.5, 98, 103) cm

Next row: BO 5 (5, 6, 6, 6, 7) sts, work to 2 sts before next edge, p2tog; on other side, BO 1 st, work to end.

Next row: BO 5 (5, 5, 6, 6, 6) sts, work to 2 sts before neck edge, k2tog; on other side, BO 1 st, work to end.

Next row: BO 5 (5, 5, 6, 6, 6) sts, work to neck edge; on other side, work to end.

BO 5 (5, 5, 5, 5, 6) sts at beg of next 2 rows.

FRONT

Work front as for back until armhole measures 1¼ (1½, 2, 2¼, 2¾, 3¼)" (3 [4, 5, 6, 7, 8] cm), ending with a WS row.

Next row: (RS) K22 (22, 23, 24, 24, 26), place center 12 (14, 16, 16, 18, 18) sts onto st holder for neck, join a second ball of yarn and knit to end. Continue each side separately.

BO every other row at neck edge 3 sts once, 2 sts once, then 1 st twice—15 (15, 16, 17, 17, 19) sts rem each side. Work even until armhole measures 6¼ (6¾, 7, 7½, 7¾, 8¼)″ (16 [17, 18, 19, 20, 21] cm), ending with a WS row.

BO 7 sts at beg of next 0 (0, 0, 0, 0, 2) rows, 6 sts at beg of next 0 (0, 2, 4, 4, 4) rows, then 5 sts at beg of next 6 (6, 4, 2, 2, 0) rows.

FLOWER

With smaller needles, CO 66 sts. Work in garter st for 11 rows.

Next (dec) row: K1, *k2tog; rep from * to last st, k1—34 sts.

Rep dec row every row twice more—10 sts rem.

Cut yarn and pull tail through rem sts. Sew side edges tog. Sew button to center of flower.

FINISHING

Weave in ends. Block pieces to finished measurements.

Sew right shoulder seam.

Neckband

With smaller needles and RS facing, pick up and k28 sts along left front neck, knit 12 (14, 16, 16, 18, 18) sts from holder at front neck, pick up and k32 sts along right neck edge, knit 22 (24, 26, 26, 28, 28) sts from holder at back neck, pick up and k4 sts along left back neck—98 (102, 106, 106, 110, 110) sts.

Knit 7 rows. BO all sts, making sure sts are not too loose.

Sew left shoulder and neckband. Sew side seams. Sew flower to right shoulder.

Cabled Cap, Cowl, Wrist Warmers, and Knee Socks

This four-piece set will warm you beautifully on icy winter days. The lovely cable pattern isn't hard to knit, although it will take some time.

Photo page 22

finished measurements

CAP // 16½" (42 cm) circumference and 10¾" (27.5 cm) long.

COWL // 21" (53.5 cm) neck circumference and 14" (35.5 cm) long.

WRIST WARMERS // 5¾" (14.5 cm) circumference and 5½" (14 cm) long.

KNEE SOCKS // 7¾ (8¼, 8½)" (19.5 [21, 21.5] cm) foot circumference and 20½ (21¾, 22½)" (52 [55, 57.5] cm) length to heel. Shown in size 8¼" (21 cm).

yarn

Baby weight (fine #2).

Marks & Kattens Eco Baby Wool (100% eco-wool; 91 yd [83 m]/25 g): gray 172, 3 balls for cap, 7 balls for cowl, 2 balls for wrist warmers, and 8 (9, 10) balls for knee socks.

needles

CAP // U.S. size 2.5 (3 mm) needles. U.S. size 6 (4 mm) needles.

COWL // U.S. size 6 (4 mm): 24" (60 cm) and 32" (80 cm) long circular (cir) needles.

WRIST WARMERS // U.S. size 2.5 (3 mm): set of 5 double-pointed needles (dpn).

KNEE SOCKS // U.S. size 1.5 (2.5 mm): set of 5 double-pointed needles. U.S. size 2.5 (3 mm): set of 5 double-pointed needles.

Adjust needle sizes if necessary to obtain the correct gauge.

notions

Cable needle (cn); stitch markers; tapestry needle.

gauge

28 sts and 39 rows = 4" (10 cm) in St st on U.S. size 2.5 (3 mm) needles.

25 sts and 34 rows = 4" (10 cm) in St st on U.S. size 6 (4 mm) needles.

18 sts of Patt 3 Cable = 2¼" (5.5 cm) wide on U.S. size 2.5 (3 mm) needles and 2½" (6.5 cm) wide on U.S. size 6 (4 mm) needles.

STITCH GUIDE

2 over 2 Left Cross (2/2 LC)
Sl next 2 sts to cn and hold in front, k2 from left needle, k2 from cn.

2 over 2 Right Cross (2/2 RC)
Sl next 2 sts to cn and hold in back, k2 from left needle, k2 from cn.

3 over 1 Left Cross Purl (3/1 LCP)
Sl 3 sts to cn and hold in front, p1 from left needle, k3 from cn.

3 over 1 Right Cross Purl (3/1 RCP)
Sl next st to cn and hold in back, k3 from left needle, p1 from cn.

3 over 3 Left Cross (3/3 LC)
Sl next 3 sts to cn and hold in front, k3 from left needle, k3 from cn.

CAP

With smaller needles, CO 110 sts. Work in k1, p1 rib for 9 rows and inc 20 sts evenly spaced across last row—130 sts.

Change to larger needles.

Row 1: (RS) K1 (edge st), *work 4 sts in Row 1 of Left Cross Cable chart, p2, 4 sts in Row 1 of Right Cross Cable chart, p2, 18 sts in Row 1 of Diamond Cable chart, p2; rep from * to last st, k1 (edge st).

Row 2: K1 (edge st), *k2, work 18 sts in Row 2 of Diamond Cable chart, k2, 4 sts in Row 2 of Right Cross Cable chart, k2, 4 sts in Row 2 of Left Cross Cable chart; rep from * to last st, k1 (edge st).

Continue in established patt until piece measures 10¼" (26 cm) from beg, ending with a WS row.

Shape top
Next (dec) row: (RS) K1 (edge st), (k2tog) to last st, k1 (edge st)—66 sts.

Next row: K1 (edge st), purl to last st, k1 (edge st).

Rep dec row once more—34 sts.

Next (dec) row: (WS) K1 (edge st), (p2tog) to last st, k1 (edge st)—18 sts.

Cut yarn, draw tail through rem sts, and pull tight to secure.

Finishing
Weave in ends. Sew side seam.

COWL

With longer cir needle, CO 265 sts. Join to work in the rnd, being careful not to twist sts. Place marker (pm) for beg of rnd.

Rnd 1: *Work 4 sts in Row 1 of Left Cross Cable chart, p9, 4 sts in Row 1 of Right Cross Cable chart, p9, 18 sts in Row 1 of Diamond Cable chart, p9; rep from * around.

Continue in established patt until piece measures 2" (5 cm) from beg.

Next (dec) rnd: *Work 4 sts in patt, p2tog, work 11 sts in patt, p2tog, work 25 sts in patt, p2tog, p7; rep from * around—250 sts.

Work 13 rnds even.

Next (dec) rnd: *Work 4 sts in patt, p2tog, work 10 sts in patt, p2tog, work 24 sts in patt, p2tog, p6; rep from * around—235 sts.

Rep dec rnd every 14 rnds 5 more times, with 1 fewer st between dec each time—160 sts. Change to shorter cir needle when there are too few sts to work comfortably on the longer cir needle.

Continue even until 28-row rep of Diamond Cable chart has been worked 4 times.

Next (dec) rnd: Knit and dec 36 sts evenly around—124 sts.

Next rnd: Purl.

Next rnd: Knit.

Rep last 2 rnds once more, then rep purl rnd once more.

BO loosely knitwise.

Finishing

Weave in ends.

WRIST WARMERS (make 2)

With dpn, CO 56 sts. Divide sts evenly over 4 dpn (14 sts per needle). Join, being careful not to twist sts. Place marker (pm) for beg of rnd.

Rnd 1: *P4, work next 4 sts in Row 1 of Left Cross Cable chart, p2, work next 4 sts in Row 1 of Right Cross Cable chart; rep from * around. Continue in established patt until piece measures 5½" (14 cm) from beg. BO loosely in patt.

Weave in ends.

KNEE SOCKS (make 2)

With smaller dpn, CO 84 (92, 100) sts and divide sts evenly over 4 dpn (21 [23, 25] sts on each needle). Join, being careful not to twist sts. Place marker (pm) for beg of rnd (center back).

Rnd 1: K1, *p2, k2; rep from * to last 3 sts, p2, k1.

Rep rnd 1 until piece measures 4" (10 cm) from beg. Change to larger dpn.

Next (inc) rnd: Knit and inc 14 (14, 16) sts evenly spaced—98 (106, 116) sts.

Next rnd: K1, p1 (5, 2), work next 94 (94, 110) sts in Row 1 of Sock chart, p1 (5, 2), k1.

Continue even until piece measures 7" (18 cm) from beg.

Next (dec) rnd: Ssk, work in established patt to last 2 sts, k2tog—2 sts dec'd.

Rep dec rnd every 8 rnds 6 (7, 8) more times, then every 4 rnds 9 times—66 (72, 80) sts.

Work even until piece measures 18 (19, 19¾)" (46 [48, 50] cm) from beg.

Next (dec) rnd: Knit and dec 10 (12, 18) sts evenly around—56 (60, 62) sts rem.

Knit 1 rnd even.

Divide rem sts with 14 (15, 15) sts each on Needles 1 and 3 and 14 (15, 16) sts each on Needles 2 and 4.

Heel flap

Next (dec) row: (RS) Knit to last 2 sts on Needle 1, k2tog, turn—1 st dec'd. Purl sts on Needle 1, then purl to end of Needle 4, turn.

Continue in St st over 27 (29, 30) sts on Needles 1 and 4 for 19 (21, 21) more rows.

Next (inc) row: (WS) Purl to last st on Needle 1, M1, k1—1 st inc'd.

Heel

Row 1: (RS) K18 (19, 19), ssk, k1, turn.

Row 2: (WS) Sl 1, p10 (9, 8), p2tog, p1, turn.

Row 3: Sl 1, k9 (9, 8) sts, ssk, k1, turn.

Row 4: Sl 1, p9 (9, 8) sts, p2tog, p1, turn.

Rep Rows 3 and 4 until all heel sts have been used up—12 (12, 11) sts rem. Cut yarn.

Next row: (RS) Needle 4, knit 6 heel sts; Needle 1, knit 6 (6, 5) heel sts, then pick up and knit 13 (14, 15) sts along left side of heel flap; Needles 2 and 3, knit; Needle 4, pick up and knit 14 (14, 15) sts along right side of heel flap, knit 6 (6, 5) heel sts— 66 (70, 72) sts. Join to work in the rnd. Pm for beg of rnd.

Knit 1 rnd.

Next (dec) rnd: Needle 1, knit to last 2 sts, k2tog; Needles 2 and 3, knit; Needle 4, ssk, then knit to end—2 sts dec'd.

Rep dec rnd every other rnd 5 more times—54 (58, 60) sts rem.

Divide rem sts evenly over 4 dpn. Continue in St st until foot measures 7¾ (8¼, 8¾)" (20 [21, 22] cm) from heel.

Shape toe

Next (dec) rnd: Needle 1, knit to last 3 sts, ssk, k1; Needle 2, k1, k2tog, knit to end; Needle 3, knit to last 3 sts, ssk, k1; Needle 4, k1, k2tog, knit to end—4 sts dec'd.

Rep dec rnd every other rnd 5 (6, 6) more times, then every rnd 4 (4, 5) times—14 (14, 12) sts rem.

Next (dec) rnd: (K2tog) 7 (7, 6) times—7 (7, 6) sts rem. Cut yarn, draw tail through rem sts, and pull tight to secure.

Weave in ends.

Diamond Cable

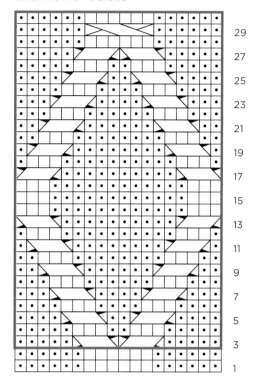

29
27
25
23
21
19
17
15
13
11
9
7
5
3
1

18 sts

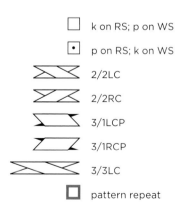

k on RS; p on WS

p on RS; k on WS

2/2LC

2/2RC

3/1LCP

3/1RCP

3/3LC

pattern repeat

Left Cross Cable

Right Cross Cable

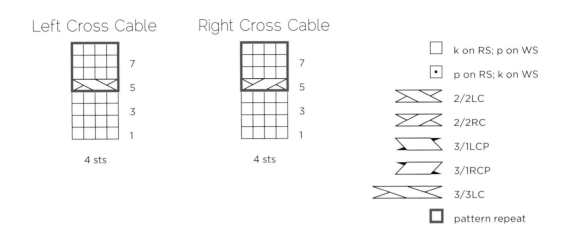

4 sts

4 sts

☐ k on RS; p on WS

• p on RS; k on WS

2/2LC

2/2RC

3/1LCP

3/1RCP

3/3LC

☐ pattern repeat

Sock

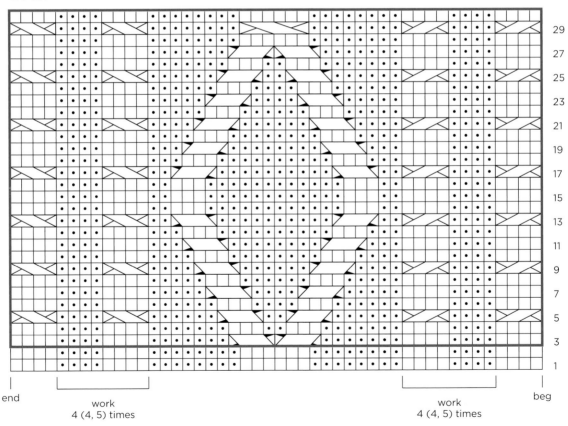

29
27
25
23
21
19
17
15
13
11
9
7
5
3
1

end

work
4 (4, 5) times

work
4 (4, 5) times

beg

shades of winter

Coat with Relief Stitch Borders

This coat has a lovely relief stitch border on the lower edge and the collar. It will be both beautiful and cozy in the fall or on cool summer evenings.

Photo page 23

finished measurements

34½ (37¾, 40¾, 45, 48, 52¼)" (87.5 [96, 103.5, 114.5, 122, 132.5] cm) bust circumference and 31½ (32¼, 33, 33¾, 34¾, 35½)" (80 [82, 84, 86, 88, 90] cm) long. To fit woman's sizes x-small (small, medium, large, 1X, 2X). Shown in size medium.

yarn

Worsted weight (medium #4).

Marks & Kattens Eco Wool (100% eco-wool, 88 yd [80 m]/50 g): gray 1978, 14 (15, 16, 17, 18, 19) balls.

needles

U.S. size 10½ (6.5 mm) needles.

Adjust needle size if necessary to obtain the correct gauge.

notions

Stitch holders; tapestry needle; two 1" (25 mm) buttons.

gauge

15½ sts and 20 rows = 4" (10 cm) in St st.

STITCH GUIDE

Double Seed Stitch

Row 1: (RS) *P1, k1; rep from *.

Rows 2 and 4: Knit the knit sts and purl the purl sts.

Row 3: *K1, p1; rep from *.

Rep Rows 1–4 for patt.

BACK

CO 87 (91, 99, 107, 115, 123) sts. Knit 1 WS row.

Work 4 rows of Double Seed St.

Next (dec) row: (RS) Work 1 st, ssk, work in established patt to last 3 sts, k2tog, work last st—2 sts dec'd.

Rep dec row every 6 rows 5 (4, 3, 3, 2, 3) times, then every 4 rows 8 (10, 12, 13, 15, 14) times—59 (61, 67, 73, 79, 87) sts. AT THE SAME TIME, when 10 rows of Double Seed St have been worked, work 7 rows of St st, knit 1 WS row, then work 20 rows of Slip St chart, beg at your size at right side of chart and keeping 1 edge st at beg and end of row in garter st (knit every row). Continue in St st until piece measures 15¼ (15¾, 16¼, 17, 17¼, 17¾)" (39 [40, 41, 43, 44, 45] cm) from beg, ending with a WS row.

Next (inc) row: (RS) K1 (edge st), M1, knit to last st, M1, k1 (edge st)—2 sts inc'd.

Rep inc row every 8 (6, 6, 6, 6, 6) rows 4 (6, 6, 3, 3, 3) times, then every 4 rows 0 (0, 0, 4, 4, 4) times—69 (75, 81, 89, 95, 103) sts. Work even until piece measures 23½ (24, 24½, 24¾, 25¼, 25½)" (60 [61, 62, 63, 64, 65] cm) from beg, ending with a WS row.

Shape armholes

BO 7 (8, 8, 10, 10, 11) sts at beg of next 2 rows, 3 sts at beg of next 0 (0, 0, 0, 2, 2) rows, 2 sts at beg of next 2 rows, then 1 st at beg of next 2 (4, 6, 6, 4, 6) rows—49 (51, 55, 59, 61, 65) sts rem.

Work even until armhole measures 7 (7½, 7¾, 8¼, 8¾, 9)" (18 [19, 20, 21, 22, 23] cm), ending with a WS row.

Shape shoulders and neck

Next row: (RS) BO 7 (7, 8, 9, 9, 10) sts, k14 (15, 17, 18, 19, 21) sts, place center 21 (21, 21, 23, 23, 23) sts onto holder for neck, join a second ball of yarn and work to end. Work each side separately.

Next row: BO 7 (7, 8, 9, 9, 10) sts, purl to 2 sts before neck edge, p2tog; on other side, BO 1 st, purl to end.

BO 6 (7, 8, 8, 9, 10) sts at beg of next 2 rows.

LEFT FRONT

CO 47 (49, 53, 57, 61, 65) sts. Knit 1 WS row.

Work 10 rows Double Seed St inside edge sts.

Next (dec) row: (RS) Work 1 st, ssk, work in established patt to end—1 st dec'd.

Rep dec row every 6 rows 5 (4, 3, 3, 2, 3) times, then every 4 rows 8 (10, 12, 13, 15, 14) times—33 (34, 37, 40, 43, 47) sts. AT THE SAME TIME, when Double Seed St is complete, on next RS row, work as foll: Knit to last 7 sts, work rem sts in Double Seed St.

Next row: (WS) Work 7 sts in Double Seed St, purl to last st, k1 (edge st).

Work 5 more rows as established.

Next row: (WS) Work 7 sts in Double Seed St, knit to end.

Next row: (RS) K1 (edge st), beg at your size on Slip St chart and work Row 1 to last 7 sts, work rem sts in Double Seed St.

Next row: (WS) Work 7 sts in Double Seed St, beg at marked st of chart and work Row 2 to last st, k1 (edge st).

Work rem 18 rows of Slip St chart, then work in St st, keeping 7 sts at front edge in Double Seed St and edge st in garter st, continue until piece measures 15¼ (15¾, 16¼, 17, 17¼, 17¾)" (39 [40, 41, 43, 44, 45] cm) from beg, ending with a WS row.

Next (inc) row: (RS) K1 (edge st), M1, knit to last 7 sts, work rem sts in Double Seed St.

Rep inc row every 8 (6, 6, 6, 6, 6) rows 4 (6, 6, 3, 3, 3) times, then every 4 rows 0 (0, 0, 4, 4, 4) times—38 (41, 44, 48, 51, 55) sts. Work even until piece measures 23½ (24, 24½, 24¾, 25¼, 25½)" (60 [61, 62, 63, 64, 65] cm) from beg, ending with a WS row.

Shape armhole

BO at beg of RS rows 7 (8, 8, 10, 10, 11) sts once, 3 sts 0 (0, 0, 0, 1, 1) time, 2 sts once, then 1 st 1 (2, 3, 3, 2, 3) time(s)—28 (29, 31, 33, 34, 36) sts.

Work even until armhole measures 3½ (4, 4¼, 4¾, 5, 6¼)" (9 [10, 11, 12, 13, 16] cm), ending with a RS row.

Shape neck

Next row: (WS) Work first 11 (11, 11, 12, 12, 12) sts and place onto holder, then work to end—17 (18, 20, 21, 22, 24) sts. Work 1 row even.

BO at beg of WS rows 2 sts once, then 1 st twice—13 (14, 16, 17, 18, 20) sts. Work even until armhole measures 7 (7½, 7¾, 8¼, 8¾, 9)" (18 [19, 20, 21, 22, 23] cm), ending with a WS row.

BO at beg of RS rows 7 (7, 8, 9, 9, 10) sts once, then 6 (7, 8, 8, 9, 10) sts once.

RIGHT FRONT

CO 47 (49, 53, 57, 61, 65) sts. Knit 1 WS row.

Work 10 rows Double Seed St inside edge sts.

Next (dec) row: (RS) Work to last 3 sts, k2tog, k1 (edge st)—1 st dec'd.

Rep dec row every 6 rows 5 (4, 3, 3, 2, 3) times, then every 4 rows 8 (10, 12, 13, 15, 14) times—33 (34, 37, 40, 43, 47) sts. AT THE SAME TIME, when Double Seed St is complete, on next RS row, work as foll: Work 7 sts in Double Seed St, knit to end.

Next row: K1 (edge st), purl to last 7 sts, work rem 7 sts in Double Seed St.

Work 5 more rows as established.

Next row: (WS) Knit to last 7 sts, work rem 7 sts in Double Seed St.

Next row: (RS) Work 7 sts in Double Seed St, beg at marked st on Slip St chart and work Row 1 to last st, k1 (edge st).

Next row: (WS) K1 (edge st), beg at your size on left side of chart and work Row 2 to last 7 sts, work to end in Double Seed St.

Work rem 18 rows of Slip St chart, then work in St st, keeping 7 sts at front edge in Double Seed St and edge st in garter st, continue until piece measures 15¼ (15¾, 16¼, 17, 17¼, 17¾)" (39 [40, 41, 43, 44, 45] cm) from beg, ending with a WS row.

Next (inc) row: (RS) Work 7 sts in Double Seed St, knit to last st, M1, k1 (edge st).

Rep inc row every 8 (6, 6, 6, 6, 6) rows 4 (6, 6, 3, 3, 3) times, then every 4 rows 0 (0, 0, 4, 4, 4) times—38 (41, 44, 48, 51, 55) sts. Work even until piece measures 23½ (24, 24½, 24¾, 25¼, 25½)" (60 [61, 62, 63, 64, 65] cm) from beg, ending with a RS row.

Shape armhole and buttonholes

BO at beg of WS rows 7 (8, 8, 10, 10, 11) sts once, 3 sts 0 (0, 0, 0, 1, 1) time, 2 sts once, then 1 st 1 (2, 3, 3, 2, 3) time(s)—28 (29, 31, 33, 34, 36) sts. AT THE SAME TIME, when piece measures 23½ (24½, 25¼, 25½, 26½, 27¼)" (60 [62, 64, 65, 67, 69] cm)

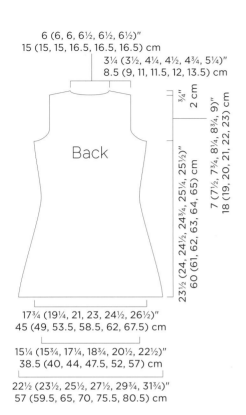

6 (6, 6, 6½, 6½, 6½)"
15 (15, 15, 16.5, 16.5, 16.5) cm

3¼ (3½, 4¼, 4½, 4¾, 5¼)"
8.5 (9, 11, 11.5, 12, 13.5) cm

¾"
2 cm

Back

7 (7½, 7¾, 8¼, 8¾, 9)"
18 (19, 20, 21, 22, 23) cm

23½ (24, 24½, 24¾, 25¼, 25½)"
60 (61, 62, 63, 64, 65) cm

17¾ (19¼, 21, 23, 24½, 26½)"
45 (49, 53.5, 58.5, 62, 67.5) cm

15¼ (15¾, 17¼, 18¾, 20½, 22½)"
38.5 (40, 44, 47.5, 52, 57) cm

22½ (23½, 25½, 27½, 29¾, 31¾)"
57 (59.5, 65, 70, 75.5, 80.5) cm

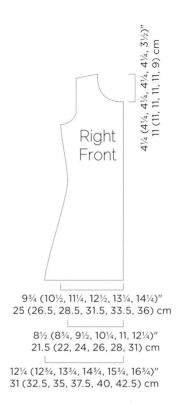

4¼ (4¼, 4¼, 4¼, 4¼, 3½)"
11 (11, 11, 11, 11, 9) cm

Right
Front

9¾ (10½, 11¼, 12½, 13¼, 14¼)"
25 (26.5, 28.5, 31.5, 33.5, 36) cm

8½ (8¾, 9½, 10¼, 11, 12¼)"
21.5 (22, 24, 26, 28, 31) cm

12¼ (12¾, 13¾, 14¾, 15¾, 16¾)"
31 (32.5, 35, 37.5, 40, 42.5) cm

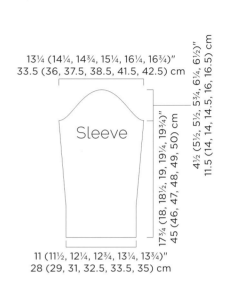

13¼ (14¼, 14¾, 15¼, 16¼, 16¾)"
33.5 (36, 37.5, 38.5, 41.5, 42.5) cm

Sleeve

4½ (5½, 5½, 5¾, 6¼, 6½)"
11.5 (14, 14, 14.5, 16, 16.5) cm

17¾ (18, 18½, 19, 19¼, 19¾)"
45 (46, 47, 48, 49, 50) cm

11 (11½, 12¼, 12¾, 13¼, 13¾)"
28 (29, 31, 32.5, 33.5, 35) cm

from beg, work buttonholes on next RS row as foll: Work 3 sts in Double Seed St, BO 2 sts for buttonhole.

Next row: CO 2 sts over buttonhole gap. Rep Buttonhole Row when piece measures 26½ (27¼, 28, 28¾, 29½, 30¼)" (67 [69, 71, 73, 75, 77] cm) from beg.

Work even until armhole measures 3½ (4, 4¼, 4¾, 5, 6¼)" (9 [10, 11, 12, 13, 16] cm), ending with a WS row.

Shape neck

Next row: (RS) Work first 11 (11, 11, 12, 12, 12) sts and place onto holder, then work to end—17 (18, 20, 21, 22, 24) sts. Work 1 row even.

BO at beg of RS rows 2 sts once, then 1 st twice—13 (14, 16, 17, 18, 20) sts. Work even until armhole measures 7 (7½, 7¾, 8¼, 8¾, 9)" (18 [19, 20, 21, 22, 23] cm), ending with a RS row.

BO at beg of WS rows 7 (7, 8, 9, 9, 10) sts once, then 6 (7, 8, 8, 9, 10) sts once.

SLEEVES

CO 43 (45, 47, 49, 51, 53) sts. Knit 1 WS row.

Next row: (RS) K1 (edge st), work Row 1 of Double Seed St to last st, k1 (edge st).

Next row: K1 (edge st), work Row 2 of Double Seed St to last st, k1 (edge st).

Slip St, back and fronts

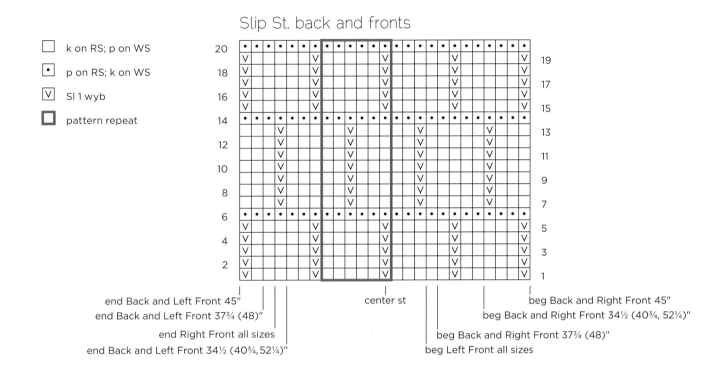

Legend:
- ☐ k on RS; p on WS
- ▪ p on RS; k on WS
- Ⅴ Sl 1 wyb
- ☐ pattern repeat

(Chart labels below)
- end Back and Left Front 45"
- end Back and Left Front 37¾ (48)"
- end Right Front all sizes
- end Back and Left Front 34½ (40¾, 52¼)"
- center st
- beg Back and Right Front 45"
- beg Back and Right Front 34½ (40¾, 52¼)"
- beg Back and Right Front 37¾ (48)"
- beg Left Front all sizes

Rep last 2 rows 4 more times.

Next row: (RS) Knit.

Next row: K1 (edge st), purl to last st, k1 (edge st).

Rep last 2 rows twice. Knit 2 rows.

Next row: (RS) K1 (edge st), beg at your size at right side of Slip St chart and work Row 1 to last st, k1 (edge st).

Next row: K1 (edge st), beg at your size at left side of Slip St chart and work Row 2 to last st, k1 (edge st).

Work rem 18 rows of Slip St chart, then beg St st, keeping edge sts in garter st. AT THE SAME TIME, when piece measures 4¾" (12 cm) from beg, end with a WS row.

Next (inc) row: (RS) K1 (edge st), M1, work in established patt to last st, M1, k1 (edge st)—2 sts inc'd.

Rep inc row every 16 (14, 14, 16, 12, 12) rows 3 (4, 4, 4, 5, 5) more times—51 (55, 57, 59, 63, 65) sts. Work even until piece measures 17¾ (18, 18½, 19, 19¼, 19¾)" (45 [46, 47, 48, 49, 50] cm) from beg, ending with a WS row.

Shape cap

BO 5 (5, 6, 7, 8, 9) sts at beg of next 2 rows, then 1 st at beg of next 2 rows—39 (43, 43, 43, 45, 45) sts rem.

Next (dec) row: (RS) K1 (edge st), k2tog, knit to last 3 sts, ssk, k1 (edge st)—2 sts dec'd.

Slip St. sleeves

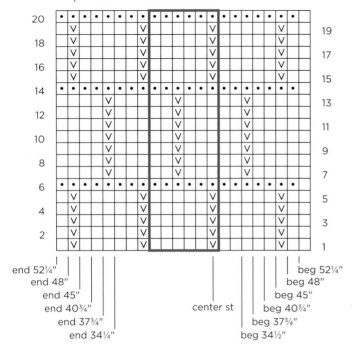

end 52¼"
end 48"
end 45"
end 40¾"
end 37¾"
end 34¼"

center st

beg 52¼"
beg 48"
beg 45"
beg 40¾"
beg 37¾"
beg 34½"

Rep dec row every 4 rows 0 (0, 0, 1, 2, 3) more time(s), then every RS row 7 (9, 9, 8, 7, 6) times—23 (23, 23, 23, 25, 25) sts. Work 1 row even.

Next (double dec) row: (RS) K1 (edge st), k3tog, knit to last 4 sts, sssk, k1 (edge st)—4 sts dec'd.

Rep last 2 rows once more—15 (15, 15, 15, 17, 17) sts.

BO rem sts.

FINISHING

Weave in ends. Block pieces to finished measurements.

Sew shoulder seams.

Collar

With WS facing, knit 11 (11, 11, 12, 12, 12) sts from holder at left front, pick up and knit 23 sts along left neck edge, knit 21 (21, 21, 23, 23, 23) sts from holder at back, pick up and knit 23 sts along right neck edge, knit 11 (11, 11, 12, 12, 12) sts from holder at right front—89 (89, 89, 93, 93, 93) sts.

Next row: (WS of collar) Work 7 sts in Double Seed St, purl to last 7 sts, work rem sts in Double Seed St.

Next row: Work 7 sts in Double Seed St, knit to last 7 sts, work rem sts in Double Seed St.

Work 1 more row as established.

Inc Row 1: Work 7 sts in Double Seed St, M1, knit to last 7 sts, M1, work rem sts in Double Seed St.

Rep Inc Row 1 every 4 rows 7 more times. AT THE SAME TIME, when collar measures ¾" (2 cm), mark center 33 (33, 33, 37, 37, 37) sts.

Inc Row 2: (WS) Work 7 sts in Double Seed St, purl to m, purl marked sts and inc 10 sts evenly spaced by pfb for each inc, purl to last 7 sts, work rem sts in Double Seed St.

Work even until collar measures 1½" (4 cm), ending with a RS row.

Next row: (WS) Work 7 sts in Double Seed St, knit to last 7 sts, work rem sts in Double Seed St.

Next row: (RS) Work 7 sts in Double Seed St, work Row 1 of Slip St chart to last 7 sts, work rem sts in Double Seed St.

Work rem 19 rows of Slip St chart, then work 4 rows of St st, keeping first 7 sts and last 7 sts in Double Seed St, work new sts into Slip St chart—115 (115, 115, 119, 119, 119) sts when all inc are complete.

Work 6 rows of Double Seed St over all sts.

BO loosely knitwise.

Sew side and sleeve seams. Sew in sleeves. Sew buttons to left front opposite buttonholes.

Wrist Warmers and Lace Socks

Wrist warmers are quick to knit and are finished with an easy crocheted edging at both ends. The lace socks go just fine with heels but can also warm your feet in ski boots.

Photo page 25

finished measurements

WRIST WARMERS // 6″ (15 cm) hand circumference and 9¾″ (25 cm) long.

SOCKS // 7¾ (8¼, 8½)″ (19.5 [21, 21.5] cm) foot circumference and 6½ (6½, 7¼)″ (16.5 [16.5, 18.5] cm) long to heel. Shown in size 8½″ (21.5 cm) circumference.

yarn

Baby weight (fine #4).

Marks & Kattens Eco Baby Wool (100% eco-wool; 91 yd [83 m]/25 g): gray, 172, 3 balls for wrist warmers and 4 (4, 5) balls for socks.

needles

U.S. size 2.5 (3 mm): set of 5 double-pointed needles (dpn).

Adjust needle size if necessary to obtain the correct gauge.

notions

U.S. size D-3 (3 mm) crochet hook; stitch markers (m); tapestry needle.

gauge

25 sts and 38 rows = 4″ (10 cm) in lace patt
28 sts and 38 rows = 4″ (10 cm) in St st

WRIST WARMERS (make 2)

With dpn, CO 54 sts. Divide sts evenly over 4 dpn, with 14 sts each on Needles 1 and 3 and 13 sts each on Needles 2 and 4. Join, being careful not to twist sts. Place marker (pm) for beg of rnd.

Purl 1 rnd. Work in pattern foll chart until piece measures 4¾" (12 cm) from beg.

Next (dec) rnd: Knit and dec 4 sts evenly around—50 sts rem.

Continue in St st until piece measures 7" (18 cm) from beg, ending last rnd 6 sts before end of rnd.

Loosely BO next 12 sts, knit to end, CO 4 sts—42 sts.

Continue even until piece measures 8¾" (22 cm) from beg. BO all sts loosely.

Crocheted edging

Rnd 1: With crochet hook, attach yarn to CO edge. Work 1 sc in each st around, ending with a sl st in first sc.

Rnd 2: Ch 6, skip 1 sc, sc in next st, *ch 5, skip next sc, 1 sc in next st; rep from * around, ending with last sl st in first ch at beg of rnd. Fasten off.

Rep edging along BO edge. Weave in ends.

SOCKS (make 2)

With dpn, CO 60 (66, 72) sts. Divide evenly over 4 dpn, with 15 (16, 18) sts on Needles 1 and 3 and 15 (17, 18) sts on Needles 2 and 4. Join, being careful not to twist sts. Place marker (pm) for beg of rnd.

Purl 1 rnd. Work in patt foll chart until piece measures 3¼ (3½, 4)" (8 [9, 10] cm) from beg.

Next (dec) rnd: Knit and dec 4 (6, 10) sts evenly spaced—56 (60, 62) sts. Rearrange sts with 14 (15, 15) sts each on Needles 1 and 3 and 14 (15, 16) sts each on Needles 2 and 4 if necessary.

Knit 1 rnd even.

Heel flap

Knit to end of Needle 1 and dec 2 (2, 3) sts evenly spaced, turn. Purl across Needle 1, purl across Needle 4 and dec 1 (2, 3) st(s) evenly spaced, turn—27 (29, 30) sts.

Work 19 (21, 21) more rows even.

Next (inc) row: (WS) Purl and inc 1 st on Needle 4—28 (30, 31) sts.

Heel

Row 1: (RS) K18 (19, 19), ssk, k1, turn.

Row 2: (WS) Sl 1, p10 (9, 8), p2tog, p1, turn.

Row 3: Sl 1, k10 (9, 8), ssk, k1, turn.

Row 4: Sl 1, p10 (9, 8), p2tog, p1, turn.

Rep Rows 3 and 4 until all the heel sts have been used up—13 (12, 11) sts rem.

Next row: (RS) Needle 4, knit; Needle 1, knit, then pick up and k13 (14, 15) sts along left side of heel flap; Needles 2 and 3, knit; Needle 4, pick up and k13 (14, 15) sts along right side of heel flap, k2tog, knit to end—68 (72, 76) sts. Join to work in the rnd. Pm for beg of rnd.

Knit 1 rnd even.

Next (dec) rnd: Needle 1, knit to last 2 sts, k2tog; Needles 2 and 3, knit; Needle 4, ssk, knit to end—2 sts dec'd.

Rep dec rnd every other rnd 6 (6, 7) more times—54 (58, 60) sts rem. Rearrange rem sts evenly over 4 dpn, with 13 (14, 15) sts each on Needles 1 and 3 and 14 (15, 15) sts each on Needles 2 and 4. Work even in St st until foot measures 7¾ (8¼, 8¾)" (20 [21, 22] cm) from heel.

Shape toe

Next (dec) rnd: Needle 1, knit to last 3 sts, ssk, k1; Needle 2, k1, k2tog, knit to end; Needle 3, knit to last 3 sts, ssk, k1; Needle 4, k1, k2tog, knit to end—4 sts dec'd.

Rep dec rnd every other rnd 5 (6, 6) more times, then every rnd 4 (4, 5) times—14 (14, 12) sts rem.

Next (dec) rnd: (K2tog) 7 (7, 6) times—7 (7, 6) sts rem. Cut yarn, draw tail through rem sts, and pull tight to secure.

Crocheted edging

Rnd 1: With crochet hook, attach yarn to CO edge. Work 1 sc in each st around, ending with a sl st in first sc.

Rnd 2: Ch 6, skip 1 st, sc in next sc, *ch 5, skip next sc, 1 sc in next st; rep from * around, ending with a sl st in the first ch at beg of rnd. Fasten off.

Lace chart

6 sts

	k on RS; p on WS
•	p on RS; k on WS
O	yo
/	k2tog
\	ssk
☐	pattern repeat

Lace Shawl with Crocheted Edging

This lace shawl has a lovely crocheted edging. It's a great choice to wear with a party dress or over your winter coat. You can wear it as a set with the wrist warmers and socks in the previous pattern.

Photo page 25

finished measurements
About 29½" (75 cm) long × 61" (155 cm) wide, including crochet edging.

yarn
Baby weight (fine #2).

Marks & Kattens Eco Baby Wool (100% eco-wool; 91 yd [83 m]/25 g): gray, 172, 13 balls.

needles
U.S. size 6 (4 mm): 32" (80 cm) circular (cir) needle.

Adjust needle size if necessary to obtain the correct gauge.

notions
U.S. size E-4 (3.5 mm) crochet hook.

gauge
24 sts and 32 rows = 4" (10 cm) in lace patt.

SHAWL

With cir needle, CO 86 sts. Purl 1 WS row.

Work Rows 1–48 of Lace chart 1, Rows 49–96 of Lace chart 2, Rows 97–144 of Lace chart 3, Rows 145–192 of Lace chart 4, then Rows 193–220 of Lace chart 5—304 sts.

Next row: (RS) K1, yo, knit to last st and dec 30 sts evenly spaced, yo, k1—276 sts.

Next row: Knit.

Next (inc) row: K1, yo, knit to last st, yo, k1—278 sts.

Rep last 2 rows twice more—282 sts.

Knit 1 row even.

BO all sts but do not fasten off last st and do not cut yarn.

Crocheted Edging

Row 1: (RS) With crochet hook and RS facing, use last st of BO row as first st, loosely work sc along edges as foll: 1 sc in each yo along left side, 1 sc in each st along lower edge and 1 sc in each yo along right side. Turn.

Row 2: *Ch 9, skip 2 sc, 1 sc in next sc; rep from * across, making sure that there are an odd number of ch-loops. Turn.

Row 3: Work 4 sl sts along first ch-loop to center of loop, (ch 3, 2 dc, ch 4, 3 dc) in first ch-loop, *ch 4, 1 sc in next ch-loop, ch 4, (3 dc, ch 4, 3 dc) in next ch loop; rep from * to last ch-loop, ch 4, 1 sc in last ch loop. Turn.

Row 4: Work 3 sl sts along first ch-loop to center of loop, (ch 3, 3 dc, ch 3, 4 dc) in first ch-loop, *ch 3, (4 dc, ch3, 4 dc) in next ch-loop, [(ch 4, 2 dc) in next ch-loop] twice; rep from * to last ch-loop, ch 3, (4 dc, ch 3, 4 dc) in last ch-loop. Fasten off.

FINISHING

Weave in ends. Block to finished measurements.

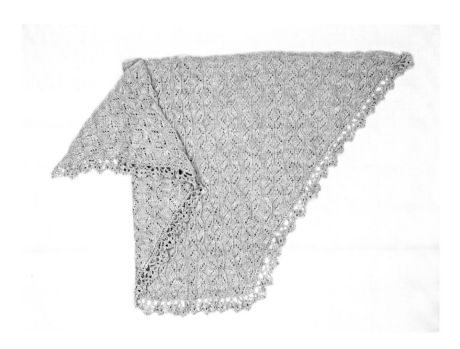

gray // lace shawl with crocheted edging

Legend

- ☐ k on RS; p on WS
- ⊡ p on RS; k on WS
- ◉ yo
- ⧄ k2tog
- ⧅ ssk
- ▣ pattern repeat

Lace chart 3

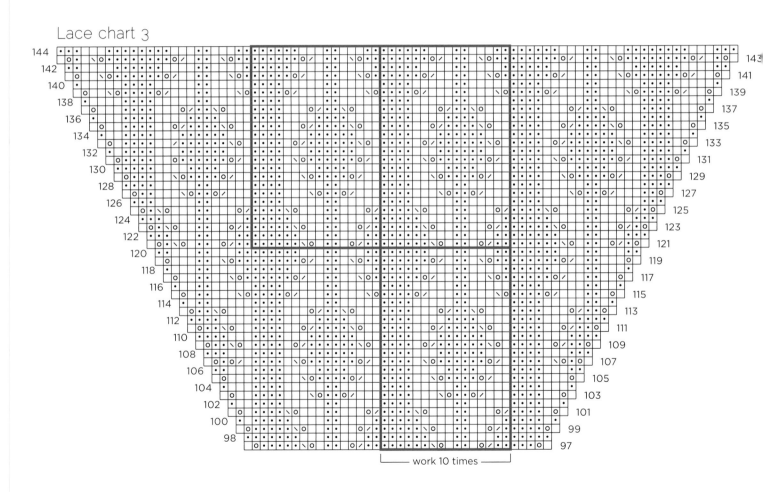

work 10 times

Lace chart 4

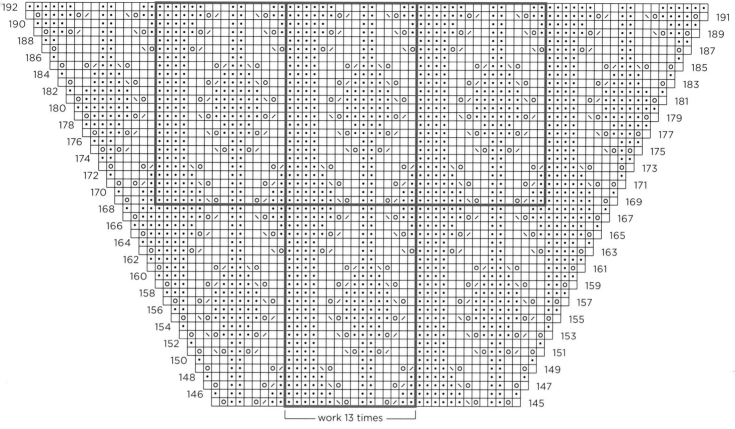

work 13 times

Lace chart 5

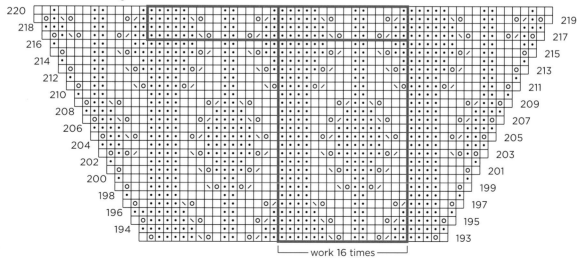

work 16 times

Lace Dress

A lacy pattern with puff sleeves, this dress is perfect to wear as a pretty tunic with jeans or leggings. The dress is worked in the round on a circular needle.

Photo page 26

finished measurements

31¼ (34, 37½, 41)" (79.5 [86.5, 95, 104] cm) bust circumference and 37¾ (38¾, 39¼, 40¼)" (96 [98.5, 99.5, 102] cm) long. To fit woman's sizes small (medium, large, 1X). Shown in size medium.

yarn

Baby weight (fine #2).

Marks & Kattens Eco Baby Wool (100% eco-wool; 91 yd [83 m]/25 g): gray 172, 16 (18, 20, 22) balls.

needles

U.S. size 2.5 (3 mm): 24" (60 cm) long circular (cir) needle.

U.S. size 4 (3.5 mm) needles.

U.S. size 6 (4 mm): straight and 32" (80 cm) and 40" (100 cm) long circular (cir) needles.

Adjust needle sizes if necessary to obtain the correct gauge.

notions

Stitch markers (m); stitch holders; tapestry needle.

gauge

23 sts and 31 rows = 4" (10 cm) in St st on size 6 (4 mm) needles.

21 sts and 33 rows = 4" (10 cm) in Patt 2 on size 6 (4mm) needles.

12 sts of Patt 1 = 2" (5 cm) wide.

Pattern 1

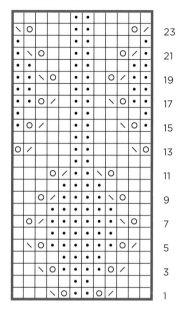

12 sts

□	k on RS; p on WS
•	p on RS; k on WS
O	yo
∕	k2tog
╲	ssk
□	pattern repeat

DRESS

With larger long cir needle, CO 250 (260, 280, 324) sts and join, being careful not to twist sts. Place marker (pm) for beg of rnd.

Rnd 1: *P13 (14, 16, 15), work Row 1 of Patt 1 over next 12 sts; rep from * around.

Work 9 more rnds as established.

Next (dec) rnd: *P2tog, p11 (12, 14, 13), work next 12 sts in established patt; rep from * around—240 (250, 270, 312) sts.

Next rnd: *P12 (13, 15, 14), work next 12 sts in established patt; rep from * around.

Rep last rnd 12 (12, 13, 13) more times.

Next (dec) rnd: *P2tog, p10 (11, 13, 12), work next 12 sts in established patt; rep from * around—230 (240, 260, 300) sts.

Next rnd: *P11 (12, 14, 13), work next 12 sts in established patt; rep from * around.

Rep last rnd 12 (12, 13, 13) more times.

Next (dec) rnd: *P2tog, p9 (10, 12, 11), work next 12 sts in established patt; rep from * around—220 (230, 250, 288) sts.

Rep dec rnd every 14 (14, 15, 15) rnds 7 more times, with 1 fewer purl st after dec each time—150 (160, 180, 204) sts rem. Change to shorter cir needle when there are too few sts to work comfortably on the longer needle.

Work even until piece measures 20 (20½, 20¾, 21¼)" (51 [52, 53, 54] cm) from beg. Change to smaller cir needle.

Pattern 2

end 34″
end 31¼ (41)″
beg 37½″

6 sts
work
12 (13, 14, 14)
times

beg 31¼ (41)″
beg 37½″
beg 34″

□ k on RS; p on WS

▪ p on RS; k on WS

○ yo

╱ k2tog

╲ ssk

□ pattern repeat

Note: When working the sleeves, if a yarnover and k2tog or ssk cannot be worked tog, work that stitch in reverse St st (p on RS, k on WS).

Next (dec) rnd: Work in k2, p2 rib and dec 6 (0, 4, 8) sts evenly spaced around—144 (160, 176, 196) sts.

Work even in rib until rib measures 3¼″ (8 cm). Divide for back and front.

BACK

With larger straight needles, CO 1 for edge st, knit first 72 (80, 88, 98) sts, CO 1 for edge st place rem 72 (80, 88, 98) sts onto holder for front—74 (82, 90, 100) sts.

Next row: (WS) K1 (edge st), purl to last st, k1 (edge st).

Next row: Knit.

Rep last 2 rows until back measures ¾″ (2 cm) from division, ending with a WS row.

Next (inc) row: K1 (edge st), M1, knit to last st, M1, k1 (edge st)—2 sts inc'd.

Rep inc row every 4 rows 8 (8, 9, 9) more times—92 (100, 110, 120) sts.

Work even until back measures 6¾″ (17 cm) from division, ending with a WS row.

Shape armholes

BO 8 (9, 11, 13) sts at beg of next 2 rows, 3 sts at beg of next 0 (0, 0, 2) rows, 2 sts at beg of next 2 (2, 4, 2) rows, then 1 st at beg of next 4 (6, 4, 4) rows—68 (72, 76, 80) sts rem.

Work even until armhole measures 7 (7½, 7¾, 8¼)″ (18 [19, 20, 21] cm), ending with a WS row.

Shape shoulders and neck

Next row: (RS) BO 6 (6, 7, 7) sts, k13 (14, 14, 15), place center 30 (32, 34, 36) sts onto holder for neck, join a second ball of yarn and work to end. Work each side separately.

Next row: BO 6 (6, 7, 7) sts, purl to 2 sts before neck edge, p2tog; on other side, BO 1 st, purl to end.

Next row: BO 6 (6, 6, 7) sts, knit to 2 sts before neck edge, k2tog; on other side, BO 1 st, knit to end.

Next row: BO 6 (6, 6, 7) sts, purl to end.

BO 5 (6, 6, 6) sts at beg of next 2 rows.

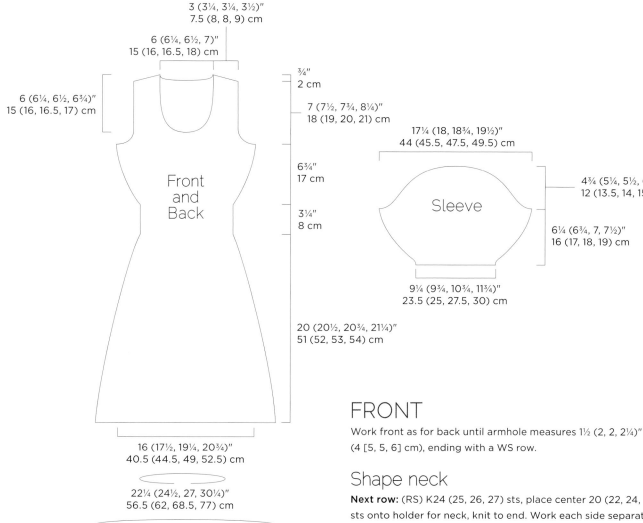

3 (3¼, 3¼, 3½)"
7.5 (8, 8, 9) cm

6 (6¼, 6½, 7)"
15 (16, 16.5, 18) cm

6 (6¼, 6½, 6¾)"
15 (16, 16.5, 17) cm

¾"
2 cm

7 (7½, 7¾, 8¼)"
18 (19, 20, 21) cm

Front
and
Back

6¾"
17 cm

3¼"
8 cm

20 (20½, 20¾, 21¼)"
51 (52, 53, 54) cm

16 (17½, 19¼, 20¾)"
40.5 (44.5, 49, 52.5) cm

22¼ (24½, 27, 30¼)"
56.5 (62, 68.5, 77) cm

42½ (44¼, 47¾, 55¼)"
108 (112.5, 121.5, 140.5) cm

17¼ (18, 18¾, 19½)"
44 (45.5, 47.5, 49.5) cm

Sleeve

4¾ (5¼, 5½, 6)"
12 (13.5, 14, 15) cm

6¼ (6¾, 7, 7½)"
16 (17, 18, 19) cm

9¼ (9¾, 10¾, 11¾)"
23.5 (25, 27.5, 30) cm

FRONT

Work front as for back until armhole measures 1½ (2, 2, 2¼)"
(4 [5, 5, 6] cm), ending with a WS row.

Shape neck

Next row: (RS) K24 (25, 26, 27) sts, place center 20 (22, 24, 26)
sts onto holder for neck, knit to end. Work each side separately.

BO every other row at neck edge 3 sts once, 2 sts once, then
1 st twice—17 (18, 19, 20) sts.

Work even until armhole measures 7 (7½, 7¾, 8¼)" (18 [19, 20,
21] cm), ending with a WS row.

Shape shoulder

BO 7 sts at beg of next 0 (0, 2, 4) rows, 6 sts at beg of next 4
(6, 4, 2) rows, then 5 sts at beg of next 2 (0, 0, 0) rows.

SLEEVES

With size 4 (3.5 mm) needles, CO 56 (59, 65, 71) sts.

Row 1: (WS) K1 (edge st), purl to last st, k1 (edge st).

Next row: K1 (edge st) *sk2p, (yo) twice; rep from * to last st, k1 (edge st).

Next row: K1 (edge st), *k1 in first yo, p1 in second yo, p1; rep from * to last st, k1 (edge st).

Next row: (RS) Knit.

Next row: Rep Row 1.

Rep last 2 rows 2 more times.

Next (inc) row: (RS) Knit and inc 28 (29, 27, 25) sts evenly spaced—84 (88, 92, 96) sts.

Next row: Rep Row 1.

Change to size 6 (4 mm) needles.

Next row: (RS) K1 (edge st), beg at your size on right side of Patt 2 chart, work 6 (2, 4, 6) sts, work next 6 sts 12 (13, 14, 14) times, work rem 4 (6, 2, 4) sts, k1 (edge st).

Next row: K1 (edge st), beg at your size on left side of Patt 2 chart, work 4 (6, 2, 4) sts, work next 6 sts 12 (13, 14, 14) times, work rem 6 (2, 4, 6) sts, k1 (edge st).

Work 8 more rows in established patt.

Next (inc) row: (RS) K1 (edge st), M1, work in established patt to last st, M1, k1 (edge st)—2 sts inc'd.

Rep inc row every 10 (12, 14, 16) rows twice more—90 (94, 98, 102) sts. Work new sts in pattern.

Work even until sleeve measures 6¼ (6¾, 7, 7½)" (16 [17, 18, 19] cm) from beg, ending with a WS row.

Shape cap

BO 7 (8, 9, 10) sts at beg of next 2 rows, then 1 st at beg of next 2 rows—74 (76, 78, 80) sts rem.

Work 2 rows even.

Next (dec) row: (RS) K2tog, work in established patt to last 2 sts, ssk—2 sts dec'd.

Rep dec row every 4 rows 3 (4, 5, 6) more times, then every RS row 8 (8, 7, 7) times—50 (50, 52, 52) sts rem.

Work 1 row even.

BO 2 sts at beg of next 4 rows. BO rem 42 (42, 44, 44) sts. Cut yarn, leaving a 12" (30.5 cm) tail.

FINISHING

Weave in ends. Block pieces to finished measurements.

Sew right shoulder seam.

Neckband

With size 4 (3.5 mm) needles and RS facing, pick up and k36 (36, 35, 36) sts along left front neck, k20 (22, 24, 26) from front holder, pick up and k42 (41, 41, 42) sts along right neck, k30 (32, 34, 36) from back holder, then pick up and k6 sts along left back neck—134 (137, 140, 146) sts.

Row 1: (WS) Knit.

Row 2: K1 (edge st), *sk2p, (yo) twice; rep from * to last st, k1 (edge st).

Row 3: K1 (edge st), *k1 in first yo, p1 in second yo, p1; rep from * to last st, k1 (edge st).

BO all sts.

Sew end of neckband and left shoulder seam. Sew side and sleeve seams.

Thread long tail through 42 (42, 44, 44) BO sts at top of each sleeve and gather to about 3½" (9 cm). Sew in sleeves.

Stockinette Dress with Garter Stitch Edgings and Buttons

This is an easy-to-knit dress with mother-of-pearl buttons sewn on around the neck and sleeves. Use your imagination and substitute other buttons or knit the flower from the pattern on page 76 to give your dress its own character.

Photo page 27

finished measurements

34¼ (37½, 40¾, 44¼, 48½, 53)" (87 [95, 103.5, 112.5, 123, 134.5] cm) bust circumference and 32½ (33½, 34, 35, 36, 36½)" (82.5 [85, 86.5, 89, 91.5, 92.5] cm) long. To fit woman's sizes x-small (small, medium, large, 1X, 2X). Shown in size medium.

yarn

Worsted weight (medium #4).

Marks & Kattens Eco Wool (100% eco-wool; 88 yd [80 m]/50 g): gray 1978, 14 (15, 16, 17, 19, 21) balls.

needles

U.S. sizes 10 (6 mm) needles.

U.S. size 10½ (6.5 mm) needles.

Adjust needle sizes if necessary to obtain the correct gauge.

notions

Stitch markers (m); stitch holders, tapestry needle; sewing needle and matching thread; forty-six (forty-six, forty-six, forty-eight, forty-eight, forty-eight) ½" (13 mm) buttons or beads.

gauge

14½ sts and 19 rows = 4" (10 cm) in St st on larger needles.

Continue in St st and rep dec row on next row, then every 8 rows 4 (4, 3, 4, 4, 4) times, then every 6 rows 4 (4, 6, 5, 6, 6) times—50 (54, 60, 66, 72, 80) sts. Remove m.

Work even until piece measures 17 (17¼, 17¾, 18½, 19, 19¼)" (43 [44, 45, 47, 48, 49] cm) from beg, ending with a WS row.

Next (inc) row: (RS) K1 (edge st), M1, knit to last st, M1, k2 (edge st)—2 sts inc'd.

Rep inc row every 4 rows 2 (5, 5, 8, 8, 8) times, then every 6 rows 4 (2, 2, 0, 0, 0) times—64 (70, 76, 82, 90, 98) sts.

Work even until piece measures 24¾ (25¼, 25½, 26, 26½, 26¾)" (63 [64, 65, 66, 67, 68] cm) from beg, ending with a WS row.

Shape armholes

BO 6 (7, 8, 10, 12, 14) sts at beg of next 2 rows, 2 sts at beg of next 2 rows, then 1 st at beg of next 2 (4, 4, 4, 6, 6) rows— 46 (48, 52, 54, 56, 60) sts.

Work even until armhole measures 6¼ (6¾, 7, 7½, 7¾, 8¼)" (16 [17, 18, 19, 20, 21] cm), ending with a WS row.

Shape neck and shoulders

Next row: (RS) K12 (12, 13, 14, 14, 16), place center 22 (24, 26, 26, 28, 28) sts onto holder for neck, join a second ball of yarn and knit rem sts—12 (12, 13, 14, 14, 16) sts rem each side. Work each side separately.

BO at each neck edge every other row 1 st twice—10 (10, 11, 12, 12, 14) sts rem each side. AT THE SAME TIME, when armhole measures 7 (7½, 7¾, 8¼, 8¾, 9)" (18 [19, 20, 21, 22, 23] cm) shape shoulders as foll: BO 5 (5, 6, 6, 6, 7) sts at beg of next 4 (4, 2, 4, 4, 4) rows, then 5 sts at beg of next 0 (0, 2, 0, 0, 0) rows.

FRONT

Work front as for back until armholes measure 1¼ (1½, 2, 2¼, 2¾, 3¼)" (3 [4, 5, 6, 7, 8] cm), ending with a WS row. Mark center 12 (14, 16, 16, 18, 18) sts.

Shape neck

Next row: (RS) Continue armhole shaping and work to marked sts, place center 12 (14, 16, 16, 18, 18) sts onto holder for neck,

BACK

With larger needles, CO 110 (114, 126, 132, 144, 152) sts.

Row 1: (WS) K23 (25, 27, 29, 31, 34), place marker (pm), k22 (22, 24, 24, 26, 26), pm, k20 (20, 24, 26, 30, 32), pm, k22 (22, 24, 24, 26, 26), pm, knit rem 23 (25, 27, 29, 31, 34) sts.

Continue in garter st (knit every row) until piece measures 1½" (4 cm) from beg, ending with a WS row.

Next (dec) row: (RS) K1 (edge st), ssk, (knit to 2 sts before m, ssk, sm) twice, k20 (20, 24, 26, 30, 32), sm, k2tog, knit to next m, sm, k2tog, knit to last 3 sts, k2tog, k1 (edge st)—6 sts dec'd.

Continue even until piece measures 2¾" (7 cm), ending with a WS row.

Next row: (RS) Knit.

Next row: K1 (edge st), purl to last st, k1 (edge st).

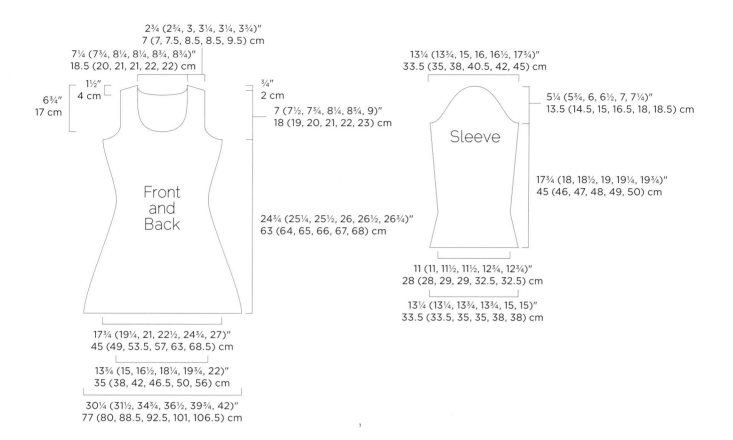

Front and Back

2¾ (2¾, 3, 3¼, 3¼, 3¾)"
7 (7, 7.5, 8.5, 8.5, 9.5) cm

7¼ (7¾, 8¼, 8¼, 8¾, 8¾)"
18.5 (20, 21, 21, 22, 22) cm

1½"
4 cm

6¾"
17 cm

¾"
2 cm

7 (7½, 7¾, 8¼, 8¾, 9)"
18 (19, 20, 21, 22, 23) cm

24¾ (25¼, 25½, 26, 26½, 26¾)"
63 (64, 65, 66, 67, 68) cm

17¾ (19¼, 21, 22½, 24¾, 27)"
45 (49, 53.5, 57, 63, 68.5) cm

13¾ (15, 16½, 18¼, 19¾, 22)"
35 (38, 42, 46.5, 50, 56) cm

30¼ (31½, 34¾, 36½, 39¾, 42)"
77 (80, 88.5, 92.5, 101, 106.5) cm

Sleeve

13¼ (13¾, 15, 16, 16½, 17¾)"
33.5 (35, 38, 40.5, 42, 45) cm

5¼ (5¾, 6, 6½, 7, 7¼)"
13.5 (14.5, 15, 16.5, 18, 18.5) cm

17¾ (18, 18½, 19, 19¼, 19¾)"
45 (46, 47, 48, 49, 50) cm

11 (11, 11½, 11½, 12¾, 12¾)"
28 (28, 29, 29, 32.5, 32.5) cm

13¼ (13¼, 13¾, 13¾, 15, 15)"
33.5 (33.5, 35, 35, 38, 38) cm

join a second ball of yarn and work to end. Work each side separately.

BO at each neck edge every other row 3 sts once, 2 sts once, then 1 st twice—10 (10, 11, 12, 12, 14) sts rem each side.

Work even until armhole measures 7 (7½, 7¾, 8¼, 8¾, 9)" (18 [19, 20, 21, 22, 23] cm), ending with a WS row.

Shape shoulders

BO 5 (5, 6, 6, 6, 7) sts at beg of next 4 (4, 2, 4, 4, 4) rows, then 5 sts at beg of next 0 (0, 2, 0, 0, 0) rows.

SLEEVES

With larger needles, CO 48 (48, 50, 50, 54, 54) sts.

Row 1: (WS) K15 (15, 16, 16, 17, 17), pm, k16 (16, 16, 16, 18, 18), pm, knit rem 17 (17, 18, 18, 19, 19) sts.

Continue in garter st until piece measures 1½" (4 cm) from beg, ending with a WS row.

Next (dec) row: (RS) K1 (edge st), k2tog, (knit to m, sm, k2tog) twice, knit to last 3 sts, k2tog, k1 (edge st)—4 sts dec'd. Remove m.

Work even until piece measures 3¼" (8 cm) from beg, ending with a WS row.

Rep dec row—40 (40, 42, 42, 46, 46) sts rem.

Work even until piece measures 5" (13 cm) from beg, ending with a WS row.

Next row: (RS) Knit.

Work 2 rows even.

Next (dec) row: (RS) K1 (edge st), k2tog, knit to last 3 sts, ssk, k1 (edge st)—2 sts dec'd.

Rep dec row every 4 rows 0 (0, 1, 1, 2, 2) time(s), then every RS row 8 (9, 8, 9, 8, 9) times—19 (18, 20, 20, 20, 20) sts rem.

Work 1 row even.

Next (double dec) row: (RS) K1 (edge st), k3tog, knit to last 4 sts, sssk, k1 (edge st)—14 (14, 14, 16, 16, 16) sts.

BO rem sts.

FINISHING

Weave in ends. Block pieces to finished measurements.

Sew right shoulder seam.

Neckband

With smaller needles and RS facing, pick up and k24 sts along left front neck edge, k12 (14, 16, 16, 18, 18) sts from holder at front, pick up and k32 sts along right neck edge, k22 (24, 26, 26, 28, 28) sts from holder at back, then pick up k8 sts along left back neck edge—98 (102, 106, 106, 110, 110) sts.

Knit 7 rows. BO all sts, making sure row is not too loose.

Sew left shoulder seam and end of neckband. Sew side and sleeve seams. Sew in sleeves. With sewing needle and matching thread, sew 18 buttons or beads around front neck, 8 (8, 8, 9, 9, 9) above each sleeve cuff, and 6 at top of each sleeve as pictured.

Next row: K1 (edge st), purl to last st, k1 (edge st).

Next (inc) row: (RS) K1 (edge st), M1, knit to last st, M1, k2 (edge st)—2 sts inc'd.

Rep inc row every 16 (12, 10, 8, 10, 8) rows 3 (4, 5, 7, 6, 8) more times—48 (50, 54, 58, 60, 64) sts.

Work even until piece measures 17¾ (18, 18½, 19, 19¼, 19¾)" (45 [46, 47, 48, 49, 50] cm) from beg, ending with a WS row.

Shape cap

BO 5 (5, 6, 7, 8, 9) sts at beg of next 2 rows, then 1 st at beg of next 2 rows—36 (38, 40, 42, 42, 44) sts rem.

Cabled Vest

Cinch this cabled vest with a wide leather belt, if you wish, and pair it with the cabled knee socks on page 80.

Photo page 28

finished measurements

29¼ (32, 35, 39, 41¾, 45¾)" (74.5 [81.5, 89, 99, 106, 116] cm) bust circumference and 29½ (30¼, 31, 32, 32¾, 33½)" (75 [77, 79, 81, 83, 85] cm) long. To fit woman's sizes x-small (small, medium, large, 1X, 2X). Shown in size medium.

yarn

Worsted weight (medium #4).

Marks & Kattens Eco Wool (100% eco-wool; 88 yd [80 m]/50 g): gray 1978, 8 (8, 9, 10, 10, 11) balls.

needles

U.S. size 9 (5.5 mm) needles.

U.S. size 10½ (6.5 mm) needles.

Adjust needle sizes if necessary to obtain the correct gauge.

notions

Stitch markers; locking markers (m); stitch holder; cable needle (cn); tapestry needle.

gauge

16½ sts and 22 rows = 4" (10 cm) in Double Seed St on larger needles.

48 sts of Center Cable chart = 9¾" (25 cm).

STITCH GUIDE

Double Seed Stitch

Row 1: (RS) *P1, k1; rep from *.

Rows 2 and 4: Knit the knit sts and purl the purl sts.

Row 3: *K1, p1; rep from *.

Rep Rows 1–4 for patt.

2 over 1 Left Cross Purl (2/1 LCP)

Sl next 2 sts to cn and hold in front, p1 from left needle, k2 from cn.

2 over 1 Right Cross Purl (2/1 RCP)

Sl next st to cn and hold in back, k2 from left needle, p1 from cn.

2 over 2 Left Cross (2/2 LC)

Sl next 2 sts to cn and hold in front, k2 from left needle, k2 from cn.

2 over 2 Right Cross (2/2 RC)

Sl next 2 sts to cn and hold in back, k2 from left needle, k2 from cn.

Notes

Markers are used to separate the Center Cable chart stitches from the stitches worked in Double Seed Stitch; slip markers every row as you come to them.

BACK

With larger needles, CO 70 (74, 82, 88, 94, 102) sts. Knit 1 WS row.

Next row: (RS) Work first 11 (13, 17, 20, 23, 27) sts in Row 1 of Double Seed St patt, place marker (pm), work next 48 sts in Row 1 of Center Cable chart, pm, work rem 11 (13, 17, 20, 23, 27) sts in Row 1 of Double Seed St patt.

Next row: Work first 11 (13, 17, 20, 23, 27) sts in Row 2 of Double Seed St patt, work next 48 sts in Row 2 of Center Cable chart, work rem 11 (13, 17, 20, 23, 27) sts in Row 2 of Double Seed St patt.

Continue in established patt, rep Rows 1 and 2 of Double Seed St, and Rows 3–38 of Center Cable chart and work until piece measures 7¾ (7¾, 7¾, 8¾, 8¾, 8¾)" (20 [20, 20, 22, 22, 22] cm) from beg, ending with a WS row.

Next (inc) row: (RS) CO 1 st (edge st), work in established patt to end, CO 1 st (edge st)—72 (76, 84, 90, 96, 104) sts. Place locking m at each end for top of slit.

Next row: (WS) K1 (edge st), work in patt to last st, k1 (edge st).

Next (dec) row: K1 (edge st), k2tog, work in patt to last 3 sts, ssk, k1 (edge st)—2 sts dec'd.

Rep dec row every 4 rows 6 (6, 7, 7, 7, 7) more times—58 (62, 68, 74, 80, 88) sts rem.

Work even until piece measures 13½ (13¾, 14¼, 15, 15¼, 15¾)" (34 [35, 36, 38, 39, 40] cm) from beg, ending with a WS row.

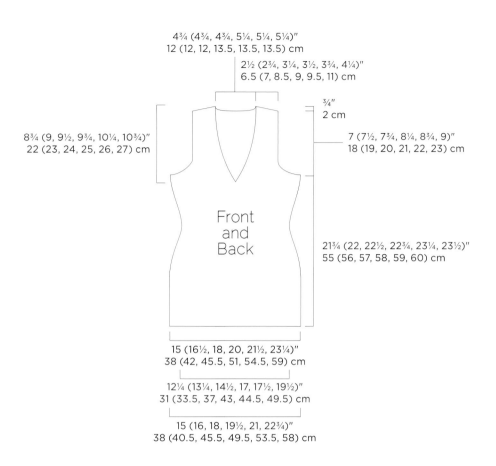

4¾ (4¾, 4¾, 5¼, 5¼, 5¼)"
12 (12, 12, 13.5, 13.5, 13.5) cm

2½ (2¾, 3¼, 3½, 3¾, 4¼)"
6.5 (7, 8.5, 9, 9.5, 11) cm

¾"
2 cm

8¾ (9, 9½, 9¾, 10¼, 10¾)"
22 (23, 24, 25, 26, 27) cm

7 (7½, 7¾, 8¼, 8¾, 9)"
18 (19, 20, 21, 22, 23) cm

Front
and
Back

21¾ (22, 22½, 22¾, 23¼, 23½)"
55 (56, 57, 58, 59, 60) cm

15 (16½, 18, 20, 21½, 23¼)"
38 (42, 45.5, 51, 54.5, 59) cm

12¼ (13¼, 14½, 17, 17½, 19½)"
31 (33.5, 37, 43, 44.5, 49.5) cm

15 (16, 18, 19½, 21, 22¾)"
38 (40.5, 45.5, 49.5, 53.5, 58) cm

Next (inc) row: (RS) K1 (edge st), M1, work in established patt to last st, M1, k1 (edge st)—2 sts inc'd.

Rep inc row every 8 (6, 6, 6, 6, 6) rows 5 (6, 6, 4, 4, 4) more times, then every 4 rows 0 (0, 0, 3, 3, 3) times—70 (76, 82, 90, 96, 104) sts.

Work even until piece measures 21¾ (22, 22½, 22¾, 23¼, 23½)" (55 [56, 57, 58, 59, 60] cm) from beg, ending with a WS row.

Shape armholes

BO 7 (8, 9, 11, 12, 13) sts at beg of next 2 rows, 3 sts at beg of next 0 (0, 0, 0, 2, 2) rows, 2 sts at beg of next 2 (2, 2, 2, 0, 2)

rows, then 1 st at beg of next 4 (6, 6, 6, 6, 4) rows—48 (50, 54, 58, 60, 64) sts rem.

Work even until armhole measures 7 (7½, 7¾, 8¼, 8¾, 9)" (18 [19, 20, 21, 22, 23] cm), ending with a WS row.

Shape shoulders and neck

Next row: (RS) BO 6 (7, 8, 8, 9, 10) sts, work 13 (14, 16, 17, 18, 20) sts, place center 22 (22, 22, 24, 24, 24) sts onto holder for neck, join a second ball of yarn, work to end. Work each side separately.

Center Cable

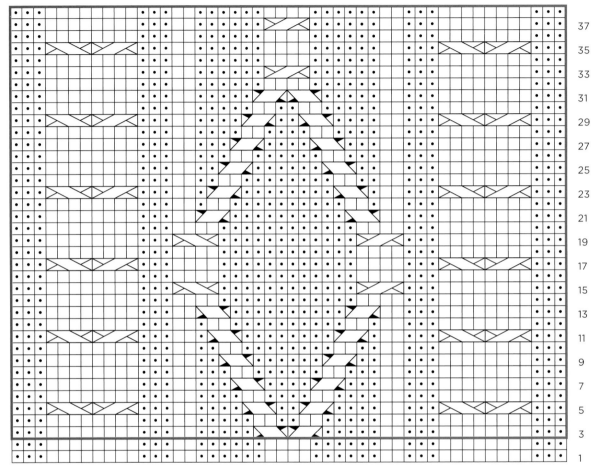

48 sts

☐ k on RS; p on WS	2/1LCP
• p on RS; k on WS	2/1RCP
2/2LC	☐ pattern repeat
2/2RC	

37
35
33
31
29
27
25
23
21
19
17
15
13
11
9
7
5
3
1

Next row: BO 6 (7, 8, 8, 9, 10) sts, work to 2 sts before neck edge, p2tog; on other side, BO 1 st, work to end.

BO 6 (6, 7, 8, 8, 9) sts at beg of next 2 rows.

FRONT

Work front same as back until piece measures 20¾ (21¼, 21¾, 22, 22½, 22¾)" (53 [54, 55, 56, 57, 58] cm) from beg, ending with a WS row.

Shape neck

Next row: (RS) Work to center of row, CO 1 st, with a second ball of yarn, CO 1 st, then work to end of row. Work each side separately and continue rem side shaping.

Next row: (WS) Work to 1 st before neck edge, k1 (edge st); on other side, k1 (edge st), work to end.

Next (dec) row: (RS) Work to 3 sts before neck edge, p2tog, k1 (edge st); on other side, k1 (edge st), ssp, work to end—1 st dec'd each side.

Rep dec row every RS row 5 (5, 3, 3, 1, 1) more time(s), then every 4 rows 7 (7, 9, 10, 12, 12) times. AT THE SAME TIME, when piece measures 21¾ (22, 22½, 22¾, 23¼, 23½)" (55 [56, 57, 58, 59, 60] cm) from beg, ending with a WS row.

Shape armholes

BO 7 (8, 9, 11, 12, 13) sts at beg of next 2 rows, 3 sts at beg of next 0 (0, 0, 0, 2, 2) rows, 2 sts at beg of next 2 (2, 2, 2, 0, 2) rows, then 1 st at beg of next 4 (6, 6, 6, 6, 4) rows—12 (13, 15, 16, 17, 19) sts rem when all shaping is complete.

Work even until armhole measures 7 (7½, 7¾, 8¼, 8¾, 9)" (18 [19, 20, 21, 22, 23] cm), ending with a WS row.

Shape shoulders

BO 6 (7, 8, 8, 9, 10) sts at beg of first 2 rows, then 6 (6, 6, 7, 8, 8, 9) sts at beg of next 2 rows.

FINISHING

Weave in ends. Block pieces to finished measurements.

Sew right shoulder seam.

Neckband

With RS facing and smaller needles, pick up and knit 34 (36, 38, 40, 42, 44) sts along left neck edge (about 4 sts for every 5 rows), pm, 2 sts at the center of the V, pm, 34 (36, 38, 40, 42, 44) sts along right front edge, 4 sts along right back edge, knit the 22 (22, 22, 24, 24, 24) sts from holder at back neck, then 4 sts along left back edge—100 (104, 108, 114, 118, 122) sts.

Next row: (WS) (K2, p2) to 2 (0, 2, 0, 2, 0) sts before m, k2 (0, 2, 0, 2, 0), p2 center sts, k2 (0, 2, 0, 2, 0), (p2, k2) to end of row.

Next (dec) row: (RS) Work in established rib to 2 sts before m, k2tog (or p2tog to maintain patt), k2, ssk (or ssp to maintain patt), work in rib to end—2 sts dec'd.

Rep dec row every RS row twice more—94 (98, 102, 108, 112, 116) sts. Work 1 WS row even.

BO loosely in rib.

Armhole bands

With smaller needles, pick up and knit 78 (82, 86, 90, 94, 98) sts along armhole edge (1 st in each st and about 4 sts for every 5 rows).

Next row: (WS) K1 (edge st), (p2, k2) to last st, k1 (edge st).

Rep last row 6 more times. BO loosely in rib.

Sew left shoulder and neckband seam. Sew side seams to slit.

Cabled Cardigan

This short cabled cardigan pairs equally well with skirts and pants. You might want to wear it with the cap and wrist warmers shown on page 80.

Photo page 30

finished measurements

37 (40, 43, 47, 52)" (94 [101.5, 109, 119.5, 132 cm) bust circumference and 19¼ (20, 20¾, 21¾, 22½)" (49 [51, 53, 55, 57] cm) long. To fit woman's sizes small (medium, large, 1X, 2X). Shown in size medium.

yarn

Worsted weight (medium #4).

Marks & Kattens Eco Wool (100% eco-wool, 88 yd [80 m]/50 g): gray 1978, 13 (14, 15, 16, 17) balls.

needles

U.S. size 9 (5.5 mm) needles.

U.S. size 10½ (6.5 mm) needles.

Adjust needle sizes if necessary to obtain the correct gauge.

notions

Stitch holder; cable needle (cn); tapestry needle; five 1" (25 mm) buttons.

gauge

14½ sts and 20 rows = 4" (10 cm) in St st on larger needles.

12 sts of Horseshoe Cable = 2½" (6.5 cm).

8 sts of Honeycomb Patt = 1¾" (4.5 cm).

STITCH GUIDE

Double Seed Stitch

Row 1: (RS) *P1, k1; rep from *.

Rows 2 and 4: Knit the knit sts and purl the purl sts.

Row 3: *K1, p1; rep from *.

Rep Rows 1–4 for patt.

1 over 1 Left Cross (1/1 LC)

Sl next st to cn and hold in front, k1 from left needle, k1 from cn.

1 over 1 Right Cross (1/1 RC)

Sl next st to cn and hold in back, k1 from left needle, k1 from cn.

2 over 2 Left Cross (2/2 LC)

Sl next 2 sts to cn and hold in front, k2 from left needle, k2 from cn.

2 over 2 Right Cross (2/2 RC)

Sl next 2 sts to cn and hold in back, k2 from left needle, k2 from cn.

3 over 3 Left Cross (3/3 LC)

Sl next 3 sts to cn and hold in front, k3 from left needle, k3 from cn.

3 over 3 Right Cross (3/3 RC)

Sl next 3 sts to cn and hold in back, k3 from left needle, k3 from cn.

BACK

With smaller needles, CO 63 (67, 73, 81, 89) sts. Knit 3 rows.

Next row: (RS) Knit.

Next row: (WS) Purl.

Work 10 rows in Double Seed St patt. Knit 3 rows.

Next row: (WS) Knit and inc 23 (21, 19, 19, 19) sts evenly spaced—86 (88, 92, 100, 108) sts.

Change to larger needles.

Row 1: (RS) K1 (edge st), k0 (0, 0, 4, 8), p0 (1, 3, 3, 3), work next 8 sts in Row 1 of Honeycomb chart, p3, next 4 sts in 2/2 LC chart, p3, next 12 sts in Horseshoe Cable chart, p3, next 4 sts in 2/2 LC chart, p3, next 4 sts in Chain Cable chart, p3, next 4 sts in 2/2 RC chart, p3, next 12 sts in Horseshoe Cable chart, p3, next 4 sts in 2/2 RC chart, p3, next 8 sts in Honeycomb chart, p0 (1, 3, 3, 3), k0 (0, 0, 4, 8), k1 (edge st).

Row 2: K1 (edge st), p0 (0, 0, 4, 8), k0 (1, 3, 3, 3), work next 8 sts in Row 2 of Honeycomb chart, k3, next 4 sts in 2/2 RC chart, k3, next 12 sts in Horseshoe Cable chart, k3, next 4 sts in 2/2 RC chart, k3, next 4 sts Chain Cable chart, k3, next 4 sts in 2/2 LC chart, k3, next 12 sts in Horseshoe Cable chart, k3, next 4 sts in 2/2 LC chart, k3, next 8 sts in Honeycomb chart, k0 (1, 3, 3, 3), p0 (0, 0, 4, 8), k1 (edge st).

Continue in est patt until piece measures 4¼" (11 cm) from beg, ending with a WS row.

Next (inc) row: (RS) K1 (edge st), M1, work to last st, M1, k1 (edge st)—2 sts inc'd.

Rep inc row every 24 rows 0 (2, 3, 3, 4) more times—88 (94, 100, 108, 118) sts. Work new sts in St st.

Continue even until piece measures 11½ (11¾, 12¼, 12¾, 13)" (29 [30, 31, 32, 33] cm) from beg, ending with a WS row.

Honeycomb

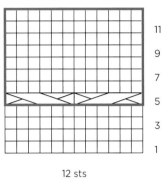

8 sts

Horseshoe Cable

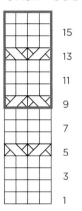

12 sts

Chain Cable

4 sts

2/2 RC

4 sts

2/2 LC

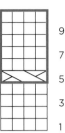

4 sts

☐ k on RS; p on WS

⊠ 1/1LC

⊠ 1/1RC

⊠ 2/2LC

⊠ 2/2RC

⊠ 3/3LC

⊠ 3/3RC

☐ pattern repeat

Shape armholes

BO 7 (7, 8, 11, 13) sts at the beg of next 2 rows, 3 sts at beg of next 0 (2, 2, 2, 2) sts, 2 sts at beg of next 4 (2, 2, 2, 2) rows, then 1 st at beg of next 4 (4, 6, 6, 8) rows—62 (66, 68, 70, 74) sts.

Work even until armhole measures 7 (7½, 7¾, 8¼, 8¾)" (18 [19, 20, 21, 22] cm), ending with a WS row.

Shape shoulders and neck

Next row: (RS) BO 10 (11, 11, 11, 12) sts, work next 21 (22, 23, 23, 25) sts, place center 20 (22, 22, 24, 24) sts onto holder for neck, join a second ball of yarn and work to end. Work each side separately.

Next row: BO 10 (11, 11, 11, 12) sts, work to 2 sts before neck edge, p2tog; on other side, BO 1 st, work to end.

BO 10 (10, 11, 11, 12) sts at beg of next 2 rows.

LEFT FRONT

With smaller needles, CO 29 (31, 33, 37, 41) sts. Knit 3 rows.

Next row: (RS) Knit.

Next row: (WS) Purl.

Work 10 rows in Double Seed St patt. Knit 3 rows.

Next row: (WS) Knit and inc 11 (10, 10, 10, 10) sts evenly spaced—40 (41, 43, 47, 51) sts.

Change to larger needles.

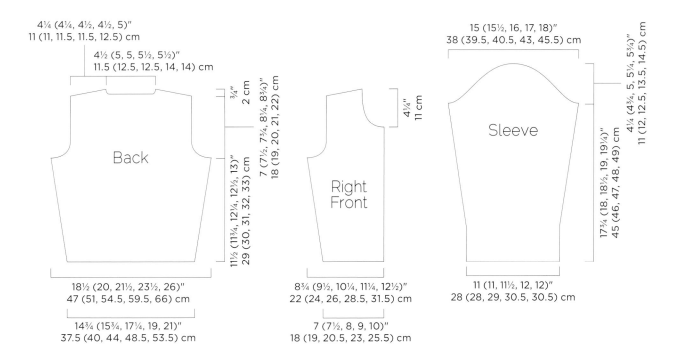

4¼ (4¼, 4½, 4½, 5)"
11 (11, 11.5, 11.5, 12.5) cm

4½ (5, 5, 5½, 5½)"
11.5 (12.5, 12.5, 14, 14) cm

Back

¾"
2 cm

7 (7½, 7¾, 8¼, 8¾)"
18 (19, 20, 21, 22) cm

11½ (11¾, 12¼, 12½, 13)"
29 (30, 31, 32, 33) cm

18½ (20, 21½, 23½, 26)"
47 (51, 54.5, 59.5, 66) cm

14¾ (15¾, 17¼, 19, 21)"
37.5 (40, 44, 48.5, 53.5) cm

4¼"
11 cm

Right
Front

8¾ (9½, 10¼, 11¼, 12½)"
22 (24, 26, 28.5, 31.5) cm

7 (7½, 8, 9, 10)"
18 (19, 20.5, 23, 25.5) cm

15 (15½, 16, 17, 18)"
38 (39.5, 40.5, 43, 45.5) cm

4¼ (4¾, 5, 5¼, 5¾)"
11 (12, 12.5, 13.5, 14.5) cm

Sleeve

17¾ (18, 18½, 19, 19¼)"
45 (46, 47, 48, 49) cm

11 (11, 11½, 12, 12)"
28 (28, 29, 30.5, 30.5) cm

Row 1: (RS) K1 (edge st), k0 (0, 0, 4, 8), p0 (1, 3, 3, 3), next 8 sts in Row 1 of Honeycomb chart, p3, next 4 sts in 2/2 LC chart, p3, next 12 sts in Horseshoe Cable chart, p3, next 4 sts in 2/2 LC chart, p1, k1 (edge st).

Row 2: K1 (edge st), k1, next 4 sts in Row 2 of 2/2 LC chart, k3, next 12 sts in Horseshoe Cable chart, k3, next 4 sts in 2/2 LC chart, k3, next 8 sts in Honeycomb chart, k0 (1, 3, 3, 3), p0 (0, 0, 4, 8), k1 (edge st).

Continue in est patt until piece measures 4¼" (11 cm) from beg, ending with a WS row.

Next (inc) row: (RS) K1 (edge st), M1, work to end—1 st inc'd.

Rep inc row every 24 rows 0 (2, 3, 3, 4) more times—41 (44, 47, 51, 56) sts. Work new sts in St st.

Continue even until piece measures 11½ (11¾, 12¼, 12¾, 13)" (29 [30, 31, 32, 33] cm) from beg, ending with a WS row and same patt row as back.

Shape armhole

BO at beg of RS rows 7 (7, 8, 11, 13) sts once, 3 sts 0 (1, 1, 1, 1) times, 2 sts 2 (1, 1, 1, 1) time(s), then 1 st 2 (2, 3, 3, 4) times—28 (30, 31, 32, 34) sts rem.

Work even until armhole measures 3½ (4, 4¼, 4¾, 5)" (9 [10, 11, 12, 13] cm), ending with a RS row.

Shape neck

BO at beg of WS rows 4 (5, 5, 6, 6) sts once, 2 sts once, then 1 st twice—20 (21, 22, 22, 24) sts rem.

Work even until armhole measures 7 (7½, 7¾, 8¼, 8¾)" (18 [19, 20, 21, 22] cm), ending with a WS row.

Shape shoulder

BO at beg of RS rows 10 (11, 11, 11, 12) sts once, then 10 (10, 11, 11, 12) sts once.

RIGHT FRONT

With smaller needles, CO 29 (31, 33, 37, 41) sts. Knit 3 rows.

Next row: (RS) Knit.

Next row: (WS) Purl.

Work 10 rows in Double Seed St patt. Knit 3 rows.

Next row: (WS) Knit and inc 11 (10, 10, 10, 10) sts evenly spaced—40 (41, 43, 47, 51) sts.

Change to larger needles.

Row 1: (RS) K1 (edge st), p1, next 4 sts in Row 1 of 2/2 RC chart, p3, next 12 sts in Horseshoe Cable chart, p3, next 4 sts in 2/2 RC chart, p3, next 8 sts in Honeycomb chart, p0 (1, 3, 3, 3), k0 (0, 0, 4, 8), k1 (edge st).

Row 2: K1 (edge st), p0 (0, 0, 4, 8), k0 (1, 3, 3, 3), next 8 sts in Row 2 of Honeycomb chart, k3, next 4 sts in 2/2 RC chart, k3, next 12 sts in Horseshoe Cable chart, k3, next 4 sts in 2/2 RC chart, k1, k1 (edge st).

Continue in est patt until piece measures 4¼" (11 cm) from beg, ending with a WS row.

Next (inc) row: (RS) Work to last st, M1, k1 (edge st)—1 st inc'd.

Rep inc row every 24 rows 0 (2, 3, 3, 4) more times—41 (44, 47, 51, 56) sts. Work new sts in St st.

Continue even until piece measures 11½ (11¾, 12¼, 12¾, 13)" (29 [30, 31, 32, 33] cm) from beg, ending with a RS row and same patt row as back.

Shape armhole

BO at beg of WS rows 7 (7, 8, 11, 13) sts once, 3 sts 0 (1, 1, 1, 1) time(s), 2 sts 2 (1, 1, 1, 1) time(s), then 1 st 2 (2, 3, 3, 4) times—28 (30, 31, 32, 34) sts rem.

Work even until armhole measures 3½ (4, 4¼, 4¾, 5)" (9 [10, 11, 12, 13] cm), ending with a WS row.

Shape neck

BO at beg of RS rows 4 (5, 5, 6, 6) sts once, 2 sts once, then 1 st twice—20 (21, 22, 22, 24) sts rem.

Work even until armhole measures 7 (7½, 7¾, 8¼, 8¾)" (18 [19, 20, 21, 22] cm), ending with a RS row.

Shape shoulder

BO at beg of WS rows 10 (11, 11, 11, 12) sts once, then 10 (10, 11, 11, 12) sts once.

SLEEVES

With smaller needles, CO 45 (45, 47, 49, 49) sts. Knit 3 rows.

Next row: (RS) Knit.

Next row: (WS) Purl.

Work 10 rows in Double Seed St patt. Knit 3 rows.

Next row: (WS) Knit and inc 7 sts evenly spaced—52 (52, 54, 56, 56) sts.

Change to larger needles.

Row 1: (RS) K1 (edge st), p1 (1, 2, 3, 3), work next 8 sts in Row 1 of Honeycomb patt, p3, next 4 sts in 2/2 LC, p3, next 12 sts in Horseshoe Cable, p3, next 4 sts in 2/2 RC, p3, next 8 sts in Honeycomb patt, p1 (1, 2, 3, 3), k1 (edge st).

Row 2: K1 (edge st), k1 (1, 2, 3, 3), work next 8 sts in Row 2 of Honeycomb patt, k3, next 4 sts in 2/2 RC, k3, next 12 sts in Horseshoe Cable, k3, next 4 sts in 2/2 LC, k3, next 8 sts in Honeycomb patt, k1 (1, 2, 3, 3), k1 (edge st).

Continue in est patt until piece measures 4" (10 cm) from beg, ending with a WS row.

Next (inc) row: (RS) K1 (edge st), M1, work to last st, M1, k1 (edge st)—2 sts inc'd.

Rep inc row every 8 rows 0 (0, 0, 4, 11) times, then every 10 rows 7 (8, 8, 5, 0) times—68 (70, 72, 76, 80) sts. Work new sts in St st.

Work even until piece measures 17¾ (18, 18½, 19, 19¼)" (45 [46, 47, 48, 49] cm) from beg, ending with a WS row.

Shape cap

BO 6 (6, 7, 8, 9) sts at beg of next 2 rows, then 1 st at beg of next 2 rows—54 (56, 56, 58, 60) sts.

Next (dec) row: (RS) K1 (edge st), k2tog, work to last 3 sts, ssk, k1 (edge st)—2 sts dec'd.

Rep dec row every RS row 4 (5, 7, 9, 10) more times—44 (44, 40, 38, 38) sts. Work 1 row even.

Next (double dec) row: (RS) K1 (edge st), k3tog, work to last 4 sts, sssk, k1 (edge st)—4 sts dec'd.

Rep double dec row every RS row 5 (5, 4, 3, 3) more times—20 (20, 20, 22, 22) sts rem.

BO rem sts.

FINISHING

Weave in ends. Block pieces to finished measurements.

Seam shoulders.

Buttonband

With smaller needles and RS facing, pick up and k67 (71, 75, 79, 83) sts from bottom of left front edge to neck (about 4 sts for every 5 rows). Knit 4 rows.

Next row: (WS) K3, purl to last 3 sts, k3.

Next row: K3, work Double Seed St to last 3 sts, k3.

Rep last row 5 more times.

Knit 4 rows. BO all sts knitwise.

Buttonhole band

With smaller needles and RS facing, pick up and k67 (71, 75, 79, 83) sts from neck along right front edge bottom (about 4 sts for every 5 rows). Knit 4 rows.

Next row: (WS) K3, purl to last 3 sts, k3.

Next row: K3, work Double Seed St to last 3 sts, k3.

Rep last row once more.

Next (buttonhole) row: (RS) K3, work 2 (1, 1, 1, 2) st(s) in patt, *BO 2 sts for buttonhole, work 11 (13, 14, 15, 18) sts; rep from * 3 more times, BO 2 sts for buttonhole, work rem 6 (5, 5, 5, 6) sts.

Next row: CO 2 sts over each buttonhole gap.

Work 2 more rows in patt.

Knit 4 rows. BO all sts knitwise.

Collar

With smaller needles and WS facing, pick up and k36 (37, 37, 38, 38) sts along end of buttonband and left neck edge, k20 (22, 22, 24, 24) sts from back holder and inc 1 st at center, pick up and k36 (37, 37, 38, 38) sts along right neck edge and end of buttonhole band—93 (97, 97, 101, 101) sts.

Next row: (WS of collar) K3 (edge sts), work in Double Seed St to last 3 sts, k3 (edge sts).

Rep last row 2 more times.

Inc row 1: K3 (edge sts), M1, work to last 3 sts, M1, k3 (edge sts)—2 sts inc'd. Work new sts in Double Seed St.

Work 1 row even. Mark center 33 (33, 33, 37, 37) sts.

Inc row 2: Work in est patt to marked sts, work marked sts and inc 8 sts evenly spaced, working inc as kf&b, work to end—103 (107, 107, 110, 110) sts.

Work 1 row even.

Rep Inc Row 1 on next row, then every 4 rows until collar measures 2¾" (7 cm), ending with a WS row.

Knit 4 rows. BO all sts loosely knitwise.

Sew side and sleeve seams. Sew in sleeves. Sew buttons to buttonband opposite buttonholes.

Sweater with Relief Stitch Borders

Enhance your wardrobe with a cozy and casual sweater with three-quarter-length sleeves. With several texture patterns embellishing its surface, this pullover is a must-have for windy fall evenings and cold winter days.

Photo page 31

finished measurements

36½ (39¾, 43, 46¼, 49¾, 54)" (92.5 [101, 109, 117.5, 126.5, 137] cm) bust circumference and 22¾ (23¾, 24½, 25¼, 26, 27)" (58 [60.5, 62, 64, 66, 68.5] cm) long. To fit woman's sizes x-small (small, medium, large, 1X, 2X). Shown in size medium.

NOTE // The sweater rolls up at the lower edge so the actual length will be about 1¼–1½" (3–4 cm) shorter.

yarn

Worsted weight (medium #4).

Marks & Kattens Eco Wool (100% eco-wool; 88 yd [80 m]/50 g): gray 1978, 14 (15, 16, 17, 18, 19) balls.

needles

U.S. size 10½ (6.5 mm) needles.

Adjust needle sizes if necessary to obtain the correct gauge.

notions

Stitch markers; stitch holders; tapestry needle.

gauge

14½ sts and 20 rows = 4" (10 cm) in St st.

STITCH GUIDE

Double Seed Stitch (multiple of 2 sts)

Row 1: (RS) *P1, k1 ; rep from *.

Rows 2 and 4: Knit the knit sts and purl the purl sts.

Row 3: *K1, p1; rep from *.

Rep Rows 1–4 for patt.

Notes

To find your starting point on each chart when working the sleeves, find the center of the first row and count back half the number of stitches on the chart to find the starting point. Work all new stitches in the established pattern as the number of increased stitches permit; in Pattern 3, if a yarnover cannot be worked with its accompanying k2tog, and vice versa, work that stitch in stockinette.

BACK

CO 68 (74, 80, 86, 92, 100) sts.

Row 1: (WS) K1 (edge st), purl to last st, k1 (edge st).

Row 2: Knit.

Rows 3–9: Rep Rows 1 and 2 three more times, then rep Row 1 once more.

Row 10: (RS) K1 (edge st), purl to last st, k1 (edge st).

Row 11: Knit.

Rows 12 and 13: Rep Rows 10 and 11 once more.

Rows 14–19: Rep Row 2 once, then rep Rows 1 and 2 twice, then rep Row 1 once more.

Rows 20–33: Rep Rows 10–19 once, then rep Rows 10–13 once more.

Work 4 (6, 8, 10, 12, 14) rows of St st, keeping 1 st at each end in garter st (knit every row).

Next (inc) row: (WS) K1 (edge st), purl to last st and inc 10 (10, 10, 12, 12, 12) sts evenly spaced, k1 (edge st)—78 (84, 90, 98, 104, 112) sts. Work inc as pfb.

Work 4 rows of reverse St st (p on RS, k on WS).

Next row: (RS) K1 (edge st), beg at your size at right side of Patt 1 chart, work 0 (3, 6, 2, 5, 1) st(s), work next 8 sts 9 (9, 10, 11, 12, 13) times, work rem 4 (7, 2, 6, 1, 5) st(s) of chart, k1 (edge st).

Next row: K1 (edge st), beg at your size at left side of Patt 1 chart, work 4 (7, 2, 6, 1, 5) st(s), work next 8 sts 9 (9, 10, 11, 12, 13) times, work rem 0 (3, 6, 2, 5, 1) st(s) of chart, k1 (edge st).

Work Rows 3–16 of Patt 1 chart as est. Work 3 rows of reverse St st.

Next (dec) row: (WS) K1 (edge st), knit to last st and dec 10 (10, 10, 12, 12, 12) sts evenly spaced, k1 (edge st)—68 (74, 80, 86, 92, 100) sts.

Work 5 rows of St st.

Next (dec) row: (WS) K1 (edge st), purl to last st and dec 1 st evenly spaced, k1 (edge st)—67 (73, 79, 85, 91, 99) sts.

Next (bobble) row: (RS) K1 (edge st), beg at your size at right side of Patt 2 chart, work 5 (1, 4, 7, 3, 7) sts(s), work next 7 sts 8 (9, 10, 10, 12, 12) times, work rem 4 (7, 3, 6, 2, 6) sts of chart, k1 edge st).

Work 4 rows of St st.

Next (dec) row: (WS) Purl and dec 8 (8, 8, 8, 8, 10) sts evenly spaced across—59 (65, 71, 77, 83, 89) sts.

Pattern 1, back and fronts

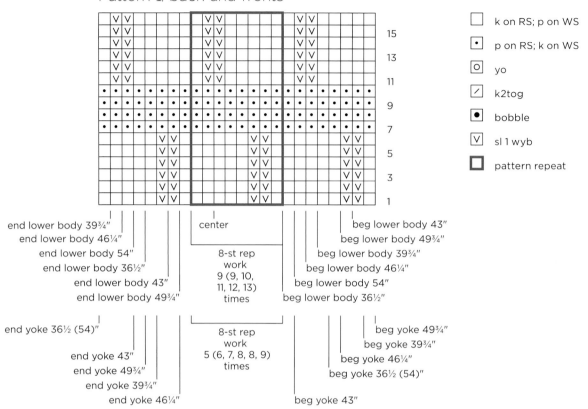

k on RS; p on WS
• p on RS; k on WS
O yo
/ k2tog
● bobble
V sl 1 wyb
☐ pattern repeat

end lower body 39¾"
end lower body 46¼"
end lower body 54"
end lower body 36½"
end lower body 43"
end lower body 49¾"

center

8-st rep
work
9 (9, 10,
11, 12, 13)
times

beg lower body 43"
beg lower body 49¾"
beg lower body 39¾"
beg lower body 46¼"
beg lower body 54"
beg lower body 36½"

end yoke 36½ (54)"
end yoke 43"
end yoke 49¾"
end yoke 39¾"
end yoke 46¼"

8-st rep
work
5 (6, 7, 8, 8, 9)
times

beg yoke 49¾"
beg yoke 39¾"
beg yoke 46¼"
beg yoke 36½ (54)"

beg yoke 43"

Pattern 1, sleeves and turtleneck

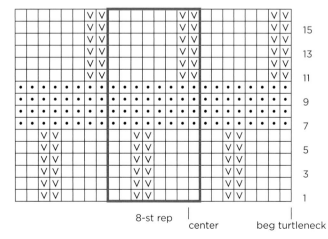

8-st rep
center
beg turtleneck

Next row: (RS) K1 (edge st), beg at arrow at right side of Patt 3 chart, work 1 st, work next 2 sts to last st, k1 (edge st).

Next row: K1 (edge st), beg at left side of Patt 3 chart, work next 2 sts to last 2 sts, work last st of chart, k1 (edge st).

Work 8 more rows of Patt 3, ending with a WS row.

Next (inc) row: (RS) Knit and inc 9 (9, 9, 9, 9, 11) sts evenly spaced—68 (74, 80, 86, 92, 100) sts.

Work 1 row of St st, 6 rows of Double Seed St, then 8 rows of St st, ending with a WS row. Piece should measure about 14¾ (15, 15½, 16, 16¼, 16¾)" (37.5 [38, 39.5, 40.5, 41.5, 42.5] cm) from beg, with bottom edge rolled.

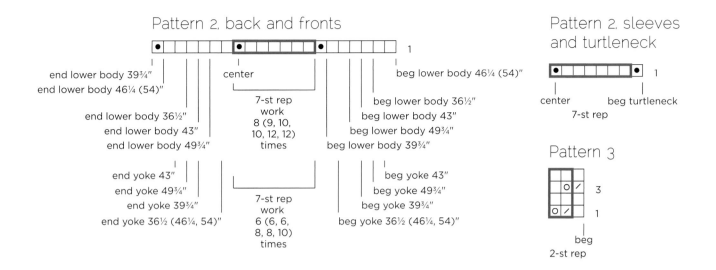

Pattern 2, back and fronts

end lower body 39¾"
end lower body 46¼ (54)"

center

beg lower body 46¼ (54)"

end lower body 36½"
end lower body 43"
end lower body 49¾"

7-st rep
work
8 (9, 10,
10, 12, 12)
times

beg lower body 36½"
beg lower body 43"
beg lower body 49¾"
beg lower body 39¾"

end yoke 43"
end yoke 49¾"
end yoke 39¾"
end yoke 36½ (46¼, 54)"

7-st rep
work
6 (6, 6,
8, 8, 10)
times

beg yoke 43"
beg yoke 49¾"
beg yoke 39¾"
beg yoke 36½ (46¼, 54)"

1

Pattern 2, sleeves and turtleneck

center   beg turtleneck

7-st rep

1

Pattern 3

3

1

beg
2-st rep

Shape armholes

Next row: (RS) BO 6 (6, 7, 7, 7, 7) sts, purl to last st, k1 (edge st).

Next row: BO 6 (6, 7, 7, 7, 7) sts, knit to end—56 (62, 66, 72, 78, 86) sts.

Next (dec) row: (RS) K1 (edge st), k1, k2tog, purl to last 4 sts, ssk, k1, k1 (edge st)—2 sts dec'd.

Next row: Knit and inc 6 (6, 6, 8, 8, 8) sts evenly spaced— 60 (66, 70, 78, 84, 92) sts.

Next (dec) row: K1 (edge st), k1, k2tog, beg at your size at right side of Patt 1 chart, work 4 (7, 1, 5, 8, 4) st(s), work next 8 sts 5 (6, 7, 8, 8, 9) times, work rem 8 (3, 5, 1, 4, 8) st(s) of chart, k2tog, k1, k1 (edge st)—2 sts dec'd.

Next row: K1 (edge st), p2, beg at your size at left side of Patt 1 chart, work 8 (3, 5, 1, 4, 8) st(s), work next 8 sts 5 (6, 7, 8, 8, 9) times, work rem 4 (7, 1, 5, 8, 4) st(s), p2, k1 (edge st).

Work Rows 2–16 of Patt 1 chart as est and rep dec row every RS row 3 more times—52 (58, 62, 70, 76, 84) sts rem.

Work 3 rows of reverse St st.

Next (dec) row: (WS) K1 (edge st), knit to last st and dec 6 (6, 6, 8, 8, 8) sts evenly spaced, k1 (edge st)—48 (52, 56, 62, 68, 76) sts.

Work 5 rows of St st.

Next (dec) row: (WS) K1 (edge st), purl to last st and dec 1 st evenly spaced, k1 (edge st)—47 (51, 55, 61, 67, 75) sts.

Next (bobble) row: (RS) K1 (edge st), beg at your size at right side of Patt 2 chart, work 2 (4, 6, 2, 5, 2) sts, work next 7 sts 6 (6, 6, 8, 8, 10) times, work rem 1 (3, 5, 1, 4, 1) st(s), k1 (edge st).

Work 5 rows in St st.

Next row: (RS) K1 (edge st), beg at arrow at right side of Patt 3 chart, work 1 st, work next 2 sts to last st, k1 (edge st).

Next row: K1 (edge st, beg at left side of Patt 3 chart, work next 2 sts to last 2 sts, work last st of chart, k1 (edge st).

Work 6 more rows of Patt 3, ending with a WS row. Work 6 rows in St st, Patt 2 chart once more, then continue in St st. AT THE SAME TIME, when armhole measures 7½ (7¾, 8¼, 8¾, 9, 9½)" (19 [20, 21, 22, 23, 24] cm), end with a WS row.

Shape neck

Next row: (RS) Work 14 (16, 18, 20, 23, 27) sts in est patt, place center 19 (19, 19, 21, 21, 21) sts on a holder for neck, join a second ball of yarn and work to end—14 (16, 18, 20, 23, 27) sts each side. Work each side separately.

Work 1 row even.

Next (dec) row: (RS) Work to 2 sts before neck edge, k2tog; on other side, ssk, work to end—1 st dec'd each side.

Work last 2 rows once more—12 (14, 16, 18, 21, 25) sts rem.

BO rem sts.

FRONT

Work front as for back until armhole measures 4¾ (5¼, 5½, 6, 6¼, 6¾)" (12 [13.5, 14, 15, 16, 17] cm), ending with a WS row. Mark center 15 (15, 15, 17, 17, 17) sts.

Shape neck

Next row: (RS) Work in est patt to marked sts, place center 15 (15, 15, 17, 17, 17) sts onto holder for neck, join a second ball of yarn and work to end. Work each side separately.

BO at neck edge every other row 2 sts once, then 1 st twice—12 (14, 16, 18, 21, 25) sts rem each side.

Work even until armhole measures 8¼ (8¾, 9, 9½, 9¾, 10¼)" (21 [22, 23, 24, 25, 26] cm). BO rem sts.

SLEEVES

CO 41 (43, 45, 45, 47, 49) sts.

Row 1: (WS) K1 (edge st), purl to last st, k1 (edge st).

Row 2: Knit.

Rows 3–5: Rep Rows 1 and 2, then rep Row 1 once more.

Row 6 (inc): K1 (edge st), M1, knit to last st, M1, k1 (edge st)—2 sts inc'd.

Rep inc row every 6 rows 0 (0, 7, 8, 10, 18) times, then every 8 rows 12 (12, 7, 7, 6, 0) times—67 (69, 75, 77, 81, 87) sts. Work inc sts into pattern. AT THE SAME TIME, continue working as foll:

Work 3 more rows of St st, 4 rows of reverse St st. Work *6 rows of St st, 4 rows of reverse St st; rep from * twice more. Work 4 (6, 8, 10, 12, 14) rows of St st, then 3 rows of reverse St st.

Next (inc) row: (WS) K1 (edge st), purl to last st and inc 7 sts evenly spaced, k1 (edge st).

Next row: K1 (edge st), work Row 1 of Patt 1 chart, counting back from center of row to find starting point on chart, k1 (edge st).

Continue Rows 2–16 as est. Work 3 rows of reverse St st.

Next (dec) row: (WS) K1, purl to last st and dec 7 sts evenly spaced, k1 (edge st).

Work 6 rows of St st.

Next row: (RS) K1 (edge st), work Patt 2 chart, counting back from center of row to find starting point on chart, k1 (edge st).

Work 4 rows of St st.

Next (dec) row: K1 (edge st), purl to last st and dec 8 sts evenly spaced, k1 (edge st).

Next row: (RS) K1 (edge st), beg at arrow at right side of Patt 3 chart, work 1 st, work next 2 sts to last st, k1 (edge st). Continue in est patt for 9 more rows.

Next (inc) row: (RS) K1 (edge st), knit and inc 8 sts evenly spaced, k1 (edge st).

Next row: K1 (edge st), purl to last st, k1 (edge st).

Work 4 rows of Double Seed St, then 6 rows of St st. Piece should measure about 16½ (16¾, 17¼, 17¾, 18, 18½)" (42 [42.5, 44, 45, 45.5, 47] cm) from beg, with edge rolled.

Shape cap

Next row: (RS) BO 6 (6, 7, 7, 7, 7) sts, purl to last st, k1 (edge st).

Next row: BO 6 (6, 7, 7, 7, 7) sts, knit to end—55 (57, 63, 63, 67, 73) sts.

Next (dec) row: (RS) K1 (edge st), k1, k2tog, purl to last 4 sts, ssk, k1, k1 (edge st)—2 sts dec'd.

Next row: K1 (edge st), p2, knit to last 3 sts, p2, k1 (edge st).

Next (dec) row: K1 (edge st), k1, k2tog, knit to last 4 sts, ssk, k1, k1 (edge st)—2 sts dec'd.

Next row: K1 (edge st), purl to last st, k1 (edge st).

Rep last 2 rows twice more, then rep dec row once more—45 (47, 53, 53, 57, 63) sts rem. BO rem sts.

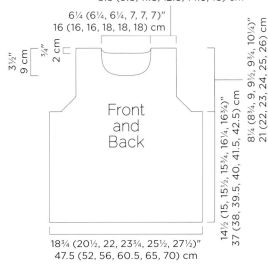

3¼ (3¾, 4½, 5, 5¾, 7)"
8.5 (9.5, 11.5, 12.5, 14.5, 18) cm

6¼ (6¼, 6¼, 7, 7, 7)"
16 (16, 16, 18, 18, 18) cm

3½"
9 cm

¾"
2 cm

Front and Back

8¼ (8¾, 9, 9½, 9¾, 10¼)"
21 (22, 23, 24, 25, 26) cm

14½ (15, 15½, 15¾, 16¼, 16¾)"
37 (38, 39.5, 40, 41.5, 42.5) cm

18¾ (20½, 22, 23¾, 25½, 27½)"
47.5 (52, 56, 60.5, 65, 70) cm

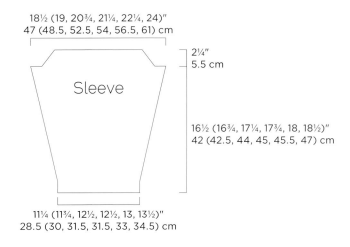

18½ (19, 20¾, 21¼, 22¼, 24)"
47 (48.5, 52.5, 54, 56.5, 61) cm

2¼"
5.5 cm

Sleeve

16½ (16¾, 17¼, 17¾, 18, 18½)"
42 (42.5, 44, 45, 45.5, 47) cm

11¼ (11¾, 12½, 12½, 13, 13½)"
28.5 (30, 31.5, 31.5, 33, 34.5) cm

FINISHING

Weave in ends. Block pieces to finished measurements.

Sew right shoulder seam.

Turtleneck

With RS facing, pick up and k14 sts along left front neck edge, k15 (15, 15, 17, 17, 17) sts from holder at front, 17 sts along right neck edge, k19 (19, 19, 21, 21, 21) sts from holder at back, then 3 sts along left back neck edge—68 (68, 68, 72, 72, 72) sts.

Row 1: (WS) K1 (edge st), purl to last st, k1 (edge st).

Row 2: Knit.

Rows 3–21: Rep Rows 1 and 2 nine more times, then rep Row 1 once more.

Next (inc) row: (RS) Knit and inc 14 (14, 14, 18, 18, 18) sts evenly spaced—82 (82, 82, 90, 90, 90) sts.

Remainder of turtleneck is worked so WS becomes RS when neck is turned to outside.

Next row: (RS) K1 (edge st), beg at right side of Patt 4 chart and work 8 sts 10 (10, 10, 11, 11, 11) times, k1 (edge st).

Next row: K1 (edge st), beg at left side of Patt 4 chart and work 8 sts 10 (10, 10, 11, 11, 11) times, k1 (edge st).

Work Rows 3–16 of Patt 4 chart.

Next row: (RS) K1 (edge st), purl to last st, k1 (edge st).

Next row: Knit.

Rep last 2 rows once more.

Next row: (RS) Knit.

Next row: K1 (edge st), purl to last st, k1 (edge st).

Rep last 2 rows once more, then rep RS row once more.

Knit 4 rows. BO all sts loosely.

Sew left shoulder and neckband seam so seam does not show when neck is turned to outside.

Sew in sleeves. Sew side and sleeve seams.

Raglan Sweater with Placket

This raglan sweater has a texture pattern around the lower edge and a placket at the neck. The soft ecological wool makes it very warm. It's a modern variation on the classic fisherman's sweater.

Photo page 34

finished measurements

37 (40½, 43½, 47, 50, 54½)" (94 [103, 110.5 119.5, 127, 138.5 cm) bust circumference and 26¾ (27½, 28¼, 29¼, 30, 30¾)" (68 [70, 72, 74, 76, 78] cm) long. To fit woman's sizes x-small (small, medium, large, 1X, 2X). Shown in size medium.

yarn

Worsted weight (medium #4).

Marks & Kattens Eco Wool (100% eco-wool; 88 yd [80 m]/50 g): beige 1980, 11 (12, 13, 14, 15, 16) balls.

needles

U.S. size 10 (6 mm): straight and 24" (60 cm) long circular (cir) needles.

U.S. size 10½ (6.5 mm): 24" (60 cm) circular needle.

Adjust needle sizes if necessary to obtain the correct gauge.

notions

Stitch holders; tapestry needle.

gauge

14½ sts and 20½ rows = 4" (10 cm) in St st on larger needles.

BACK

With smaller straight needles, CO 74 (80, 86, 92, 98, 106) sts.

Row 1: (WS) K1 (edge st), *k1, p1; rep from * to last 2 sts, k1 (edge st).

Row 2: K1 (edge st), *k1, p1; rep from * to last st, k1 (edge st).

Rows 3–5: Rep Rows 1 and 2 once more, then rep Row 1 once more.

Change to larger needles.

Row 6: K1 (edge st), k2tog, knit to end—73 (79, 85, 91, 97, 105) sts.

Row 7: K1 (edge st), purl to last st, k1 (edge st).

Row 8: Knit.

Row 9: Rep Row 7.

Next row: (RS) K1 (edge st), beg at your size on right side of body chart and work 12 (15, 18, 21, 24, 28) sts, rep next 14 sts 4 times, work rem 3 (6, 9, 12, 15, 19) sts of chart, k1 (edge st).

Next row: K1 (edge st), beg at left side of body chart and work 3 (6, 9, 12, 15, 19) sts, rep next 14 sts 4 times, work rem 12 (15, 18, 21, 24, 28) sts of chart, k1 (edge st).

Work rem 23 rows of chart as est, then continue is St st and, AT THE SAME TIME, when piece measures 4¼" (11 cm) from beg, dec 1 st on each end of next RS row as foll: K1 (edge st), k2tog, work to last 3 sts, ssk, k1—2 sts dec'd.

Rep dec row every 22 rows twice more—67 (73, 79, 85, 91, 99) sts. Work even until piece measures 17¾ (18, 18½, 19¼, 19¾, 20)" (45 [46, 47, 49, 50, 51] cm) from beg, ending with a RS row.

Shape armholes

BO 7 sts at beg of next 2 rows—53 (59, 65, 71, 77, 85) sts. Work 2 rows even.

Next (dec) row: (RS) K1 (edge st), k1, k2tog, knit to last 4 sts, ssk, k1, k1 (edge st)—2 sts dec'd.

Rep dec row every 4 rows 5 (3, 2, 0, 0, 0) times, then every RS row 10 (15, 18, 23, 23, 21) times. Work 1 WS row even.

Sizes 50 (54)" only

Next (double dec) row: (RS) K1 (edge st), k1, k3tog, knit to last 5 sts, sssk, k1, k1 (edge st)—4 sts dec'd.

Rep double dec row 0 (3) more times—25 (25) sts.

All sizes

Next row: (WS) Ssp, purl to last 2 sts, p2tog—2 sts dec'd. Place rem 19 (19, 21, 21, 23, 23) sts on st holder.

FRONT

Work front as for back until piece measures 17¾ (18, 18½, 19¼, 19¾, 20)" (45 [46, 47, 49, 50, 51] cm) from beg, ending with a WS row.

Shape armholes and neck

Next row: (RS) BO 7 sts, k33 (36, 39, 42, 45, 49), join a second ball of yarn and BO 1 st, knit to end. Work both sides separately at same time.

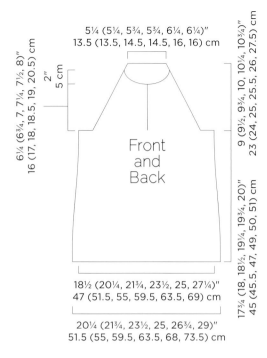

5¼ (5¼, 5¾, 5¾, 6¼, 6¼)"
13.5 (13.5, 14.5, 14.5, 16, 16) cm

6¼ (6¾, 7, 7¼, 7½, 8)"
16 (17, 18, 18.5, 19, 20.5) cm

2"
5 cm

9 (9½, 9¾, 10, 10¼, 10¾)"
23 (24, 25, 25.5, 26, 27.5) cm

Front
and
Back

17¾ (18, 18½, 19¼, 19¾, 20)"
45 (45.5, 47, 49, 50, 51) cm

18½ (20¼, 21¾, 23½, 25, 27¼)"
47 (51.5, 55, 59.5, 63.5, 69) cm

20¼ (21¾, 23½, 25, 26¾, 29)"
51.5 (55, 59.5, 63.5, 68, 73.5) cm

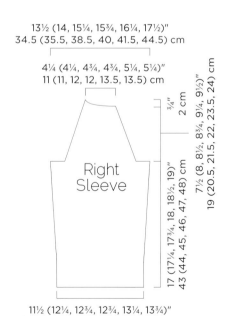

13½ (14, 15¼, 15¾, 16¼, 17½)"
34.5 (35.5, 38.5, 40, 41.5, 44.5) cm

4¼ (4¼, 4¾, 4¾, 5¼, 5¼)"
11 (11, 12, 12, 13.5, 13.5) cm

¾"
2 cm

7½ (8, 8½, 8¾, 9¼, 9½)"
19 (20.5, 21.5, 22, 23.5, 24) cm

Right
Sleeve

17 (17¼, 17¾, 18, 18½, 19)"
43 (44, 45, 46, 47, 48) cm

11½ (12¼, 12¾, 12¾, 13¼, 13¾)"
29 (31, 32.5, 32.5, 33.5, 33.5) cm

Next row: (WS) BO 7 sts, purl to 2 sts before division, k2; on other side, k2, purl to last st, k1 (edge st)—26 (29, 32, 35, 38, 42) sts rem each side. Continue 1 st at armhole edges and 2 sts on each side of front split in garter st (knit every row), work 2 (2, 2, 0, 0, 0) rows even.

Next (dec) row: (RS) K1 (edge st), k1, k2tog, knit to center; on other side, knit to last 4 sts, ssk, k1, k1 (edge st)—2 sts dec'd.

Rep dec row every 4 rows 4 (2, 1, 0, 0, 0) time(s), every RS row 8 (13, 16, 20, 20, 19) times, then work double dec every RS row as for back 0 (0, 0, 0, 1, 3) time(s). AT THE SAME TIME, after 10 (13, 15, 18, 19, 20) dec have been worked, end with a WS row.

Sizes 37 (40, 43, 47, 50)" only

Next row: (RS) K1 (edge st), k1, k2tog, knit to 6 (6, 7, 7, 8) sts before split, place last 6 (6, 7, 7, 8, 9) sts of left front and first 6 (6, 7, 7, 8) sts of right front onto st holders, knit to last 4 sts, ssk—16 (16, 17, 17, 19) sts rem each side.

Size 54" only

Next row: (RS) K1 (edge st), k1, k3tog, knit to 9 sts before split, place last 9 sts of left front and first 9 sts of right front onto holders, knit to last 5 sts, sssk, k1, k1 (edge st)—21 sts rem each side.

All sizes

Continue rem raglan shaping as est, BO at each neck edge 2 sts once, then 1 st 3 times—2 sts rem each side.

BO rem sts.

RIGHT SLEEVE

With smaller straight needles, CO 42 (44, 46, 46, 48, 50) sts.

Row 1: (WS) K1 (edge st), *k1, p1; rep from * to last 2 sts, k1 (edge st).

Row 2: K1 (edge st), *k1, p1; rep from * to last st, k1 (edge st).

Rows 3-5: Rep Rows 1 and 2 once more, then rep Row 1 once more.

Change to larger needles.

Row 6: K1 (edge st), k2tog, knit to end—41 (43, 45, 45, 47, 49) sts.

Row 7: K1 (edge st), purl to last st, k1 (edge st).

Row 8: Knit.

Row 9: Rep Row 7.

Next row: (RS) K1 (edge st), beg at your size on right side of sleeve chart and work 10 (11, 12, 12, 13, 14) sts, rep next 14 sts twice, work rem 1 (2, 3, 4, 5, 6) st(s) of chart, k1 (edge st).

Next row: K1 (edge st), beg at left side of sleeve chart and work 1 (2, 3, 4, 5, 6) st(s), rep next 14 sts twice, work rem 10 (11, 12, 12, 13, 14) sts, of chart, k1 (edge st).

Work rem 23 rows of chart as est, then continue in St st and AT THE SAME TIME, when piece measures 3¼" (8 cm) from beg, inc 1 st on each end of next RS row as foll: K1 (edge st), M1, work to last 3 sts, M1, k1—2 sts inc'd.

Rep inc row every 16 (16, 16, 12, 14, 12) rows 3 (3, 4, 5, 5, 6) more times—49 (51, 55, 57, 59, 63) sts. Work even until piece measures 17 (17¼, 17¾, 18, 18½, 19)" (43 [44, 45, 46, 47, 48] cm) from beg, ending with a RS row.

Shape cap

BO 7 sts at beg of next 2 rows—35 (37, 41, 43, 45, 49) sts.

Next row: (RS) Knit.

Next row: (WS) K1 (edge st), purl to last st, k1 (edge st).

Next (dec) row: (RS) K1 (edge st), k1, k2tog, knit to last 4 sts, ssk, k1, k1 (edge st)—2 sts dec'd.

Rep dec row every 4 rows 9 (9, 9, 9, 10, 9) times and then every RS row 0 (1, 2, 3, 2, 5) time(s)—15 (15, 17, 17, 19, 19) sts rem. Work 1 row even.

Shape neck

BO at beg of RS rows 5 (5, 6, 6, 6, 6) sts once, then 4 (4, 4, 4, 5, 5) sts once, and cont raglan dec at end of RS rows twice more—4 (4, 5, 5, 6, 6) sts rem. Work 1 row even. BO rem sts.

LEFT SLEEVE

Work left sleeve as for right until piece measures 17 (17¼, 17¾, 18, 18½, 19)" (43 [44, 45, 46, 47, 48] cm) from beg, ending with a RS row.

Shape cap

BO 7 sts at beg of next 2 rows—35 (37, 41, 43, 45, 49) sts.

Next row: (RS) Knit.

Next row: (WS) K1 (edge st), purl to last st, k1 (edge st).

Next (dec) row: (RS) K1 (edge st), k1, k2tog, knit to last 4 sts, ssk, k1, k1 (edge st)—2 sts dec'd.

Rep dec row every 4 rows 9 (9, 9, 9, 10, 9) times and then every RS row 0 (1, 2, 3, 2, 5) time(s)—15 (15, 17, 17, 19, 19) sts rem.

Shape neck

BO at beg of WS rows 5 (5, 6, 6, 6, 6) sts once, then 4 (4, 4, 4, 5, 5) sts once, and cont raglan dec at beg of RS rows twice more—4 (4, 5, 5, 6, 6) sts rem. Work 1 row even. BO rem sts.

FINISHING

Weave in ends. Block pieces to finished measurements.

Sew raglan seams.

Neckband

With cir needle and RS facing, k6 (6, 7, 7, 8, 9) sts from right front holder, pick up and k20 (20, 22, 22, 23, 22) sts along right neck, k19 (19, 21, 21, 23, 23) sts from holder at back neck, pick up and k20 (20, 22, 22, 23, 22) sts along left neck, k6 (6, 7, 7, 8, 9) sts from left front holder—71 (71, 79, 79, 85, 85) sts. Working back and forth, knit 1 row. BO all sts loosely knitwise.

Sew side and sleeve seams.

Make 2 I-cords about 7¾" (20 cm) long. Attach one cord securely at each side of neck.

Body

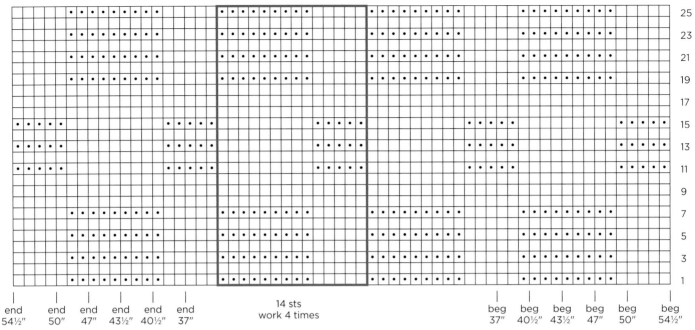

end 54½" end 50" end 47" end 43½" end 40½" end 37"

14 sts
work 4 times

beg 37" beg 40½" beg 43½" beg 47" beg 50" beg 54½"

Sleeve

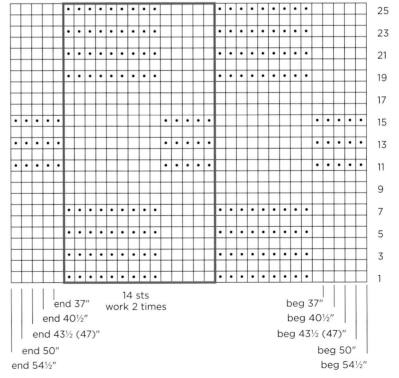

☐ k on RS; p on WS

• p on RS; k on WS

☐ pattern repeat

end 37"
end 40½"
end 43½ (47)"
end 50"
end 54½"

14 sts
work 2 times

beg 37"
beg 40½"
beg 43½ (47)"
beg 50"
beg 54½"

Sweater with Front Placket and Pockets

Here's a sturdy sweater with hidden pockets between the textured and stockinette sections. If you want a shorter front opening, you can sew down to the desired length.

Photo page 35

finished measurements

33½ (36¾, 39¾, 43¾, 47, 51)" (85 [93.5, 101, 111, 119.5, 129.5] cm) bust circumference and 30¼ (31, 32, 32¾, 33½, 34¼)" (77 [79, 81, 83, 85, 87] cm) long. To fit woman's sizes x-small (small, medium, large, 1X, 2X). Shown in size medium.

yarn

Worsted weight (medium #4).

Marks & Kattens Eco Wool (100% eco-wool; 88 yd [80 m]/50 g): beige 1980, 13 (14, 15, 16, 17, 18) balls.

needles

U.S. size 10 (6 mm): straight and 24" (60 cm) long circular needles (cir).

U.S. size 10½ (6.5 mm) needles.

Adjust needle sizes if necessary to obtain the correct gauge.

notions

U.S. size H-8 (5 mm) crochet hook; stitch holders; tapestry needle; one 1¼" (32 mm) button.

gauge

15½ sts and 20½ rows = 4" (10 cm) in St st on larger needles.

BACK

With larger needles, CO 85 (89, 97, 105, 113, 121) sts.

Row 1: (WS) K1 (edge st), k3, *p1, k3; rep from * to last st, k1 (edge st).

Row 2: K1 (edge st), k3, *p1, k3; rep from * to last st, k1 (edge st).

Rep Rows 1 and 2 until piece measures ¾" (2 cm) from beg, ending with a WS row.

Next (dec) row: (RS) K1 (edge st), ssk, work in est patt to last 3 sts, k2tog, k1 (edge st)—2 sts dec'd.

Rep dec row every 4 rows 13 (14, 15, 16, 17, 17) more times—57 (59, 65, 71, 77, 85) sts. AT THE SAME TIME, when piece measures 9½ (9½, 10¼, 10¼, 11, 11)" (24 [24, 26, 26, 28, 28] cm) from beg, change to St st. Work even until piece measures 14¼ (14½, 15, 15¾, 16¼, 16½)" (36 [37, 38, 40, 41, 42] cm) from beg, ending with a WS row.

Next (inc) row: (RS) K1 (edge st), M1, knit to last st, M1, k1 (edge st)—2 sts inc'd.

Rep inc row every 8 (6, 6, 6, 6, 6) rows 4 (6, 6, 3, 3, 3) times, then every 4 rows 0 (0, 0, 4, 4, 4) times—67 (73, 79, 87, 93,

101) sts. Work even until piece measures 22½ (22¾, 23¼, 23½, 24, 24½)" (57 [58, 59, 60, 61, 62] cm) from beg, ending with a WS row.

Shape armholes

BO 6 (7, 7, 9, 9, 11) sts at beg of next 2 rows, 3 sts at beg of next 0 (0, 0, 0, 2, 2) rows, 2 sts at beg of next 2 rows, then 1 st at beg of next 2 (4, 6, 6, 4, 4) rows—49 (51, 55, 59, 61, 65) sts. Work even until armhole measures 7 (7½, 7¾, 8¼, 8¾, 9)" (18 [19, 20, 21, 22, 23] cm), ending with a WS row.

Shape shoulders and neck

Next row: (RS) BO 7 (7, 8, 9, 9, 10) sts, k14 (15, 17, 18, 19, 21), place center 21 (21, 21, 23, 23 23) sts onto holder for neck, join a second ball of yarn and knit to end.

Next row: BO 7 (7, 8, 9, 9, 10) sts, purl to last 2 sts of left shoulder, p2tog; on other side, BO 1 st, purl to end—6 (7, 8, 8, 9, 10) sts rem each side.

BO 6 (7, 8, 8, 9, 10) sts at beg of next 2 rows.

FRONT

Worked in 2 pieces for lower section.

Right front

With larger needles, CO 41 (45, 49, 53, 57, 61) sts.

Row 1: (WS) K1 (edge st), k3, *p1, k3; rep from * to last st, k1 (edge st).

Row 2: K1 (edge st), p3, *k1, p3; rep from * to last st, k1 (edge st).

Rep Rows 1 and 2 until piece measures ¾" (2 cm) from beg, ending with a WS row.

Next (dec) row: (RS) K1 (edge st), ssk, work in est patt to last st, k1 (edge st)—1 st dec'd.

Rep dec row every 4 rows 13 (14, 15, 16, 17, 17) more times. AT THE SAME TIME, when piece measures 9½ (9½, 10¼, 10¼, 11, 11)" (24 [24, 26, 26, 28, 28] cm) from beg, BO center 21 sts for pocket on next WS row and ssk at end of row. Set rem sts aside.

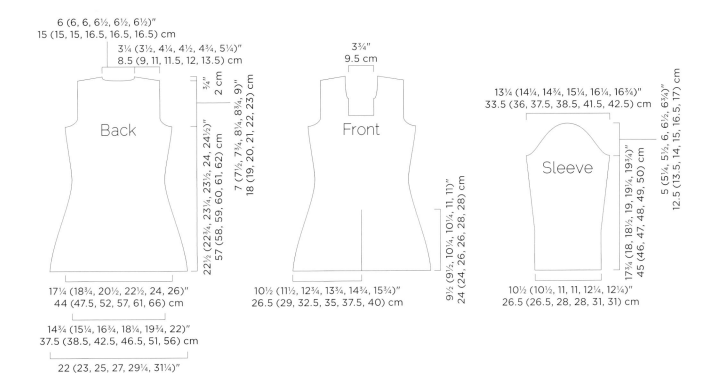

Back

6 (6, 6, 6½, 6½, 6½)"
15 (15, 15, 16.5, 16.5, 16.5) cm

3¼ (3½, 4¼, 4½, 4¾, 5¼)"
8.5 (9, 11, 11.5, 12, 13.5) cm

¾"
2 cm

7 (7½, 7¾, 8¼, 8¾, 9)"
18 (19, 20, 21, 22, 23) cm

22½ (22¾, 23¼, 23½, 24, 24½)"
57 (58, 59, 60, 61, 62) cm

17¼ (18¾, 20½, 22½, 24, 26)"
44 (47.5, 52, 57, 61, 66) cm

14¾ (15¼, 16¾, 18¼, 19¾, 22)"
37.5 (38.5, 42.5, 46.5, 51, 56) cm

22 (23, 25, 27, 29¼, 31¼)"
56 (58.5, 63.5, 68.5, 74.5, 77.5) cm

Front

3¾"
9.5 cm

9½ (9½, 10¼, 10¼, 11, 11)"
24 (24, 26, 26, 28, 28) cm

10½ (11½, 12¾, 13¾, 14¾, 15¾)"
26.5 (29, 32.5, 35, 37.5, 40) cm

Sleeve

13¼ (14¼, 14¾, 15¼, 16¼, 16¾)"
33.5 (36, 37.5, 38.5, 41.5, 42.5) cm

5 (5¼, 5½, 6, 6½, 6¾)"
12.5 (13.5, 14, 15, 16.5, 17) cm

17¾ (18, 18½, 19, 19¼, 19¾)"
45 (46, 47, 48, 49, 50) cm

10½ (10½, 11, 11, 12¼, 12¼)"
26.5 (26.5, 28, 28, 31, 31) cm

Left front

With larger needles, CO 41 (45, 49, 53, 57, 61) sts.

Row 1: (WS) K1 (edge st), k3, *p1, k3; rep from * to last st, k1 (edge st).

Row 2: K1 (edge st), p3, *k1, p3; rep from * to last st, k1 (edge st).

Rep Rows 1 and 2 until piece measures ¾" (2 cm) from beg, ending with a WS row.

Next (dec) row: (RS) K1 (edge st), work in established patt to last 3 sts, k2tog, k1 (edge st)—1 st dec'd.

Rep dec row every 4 rows 13 (14, 15, 16, 17, 17) more times. AT THE SAME TIME, when piece measures 9½ (9½, 10¼, 10¼, 11, 11)" (24 [24, 26, 26, 28, 28] cm) from beg, BO center 21 sts for pocket on next WS row and k2tog at beg of row.

Size 33½" only

Next (joining) row: (RS) Beg with left front and knit to 1 st before pocket gap, M1, k1, CO 21 sts over pocket gap, knit to last st of left front, M1, k1, CO 1 st, k1 from right front, M1, knit to pocket gap, CO 21 sts over pocket gap, k1, M1, knit to end of row.

Sizes 36¾ (39¾, 43¾, 47, 51)" only

Next (joining) row: (RS) Beg with left front and knit to pocket gap, CO 21 sts over pocket gap, knit to end of left front, CO 1 st, knit across sts for right front.

All sizes

Keeping edge sts in garter st, cont in St st and work rem dec—57 (59, 65, 71, 77, 85) sts rem when dec is complete. Work even until piece measures 14¼ (14½, 15, 15¾, 16¼, 16½)″ (36 [37, 38, 40, 41, 42] cm) from beg, ending with a WS row.

Next (inc) row: (RS) K1 (edge st), M1, knit to last st, M1, k1 (edge st)—2 sts inc'd.

Rep inc row every 8 (6, 6, 6, 6, 6) rows 4 (6, 6, 3, 3, 3) times, then every 4 rows 0 (0, 0, 4, 4, 4) times—67 (73, 79, 87, 93, 101) sts. Work even until piece measures 22½ (22¾, 23¼, 23½, 24, 24½)″ (57 [58, 59, 60, 61, 62] cm) from beg, ending with a WS row.

Shape armhole and divide front

Next row: (RS) BO 6 (7, 7, 9, 9, 11) sts, k20 (22, 25, 27, 30, 32), join a second ball of yarn to work each side of front separately, BO center 15 sts for front split, then knit to end of row.

Next row: BO 6 (7, 7, 9, 9, 11) sts, purl to split, CO 1 st for edge st; on other side, CO 1 st for edge st, purl to end of row—21 (23, 26, 28, 31, 33) sts rem for each side.

BO 3 sts at beg of next 0 (0, 0, 0, 2, 2) rows, 2 sts at beg of next 2 rows, then 1 st at beg of next 2 (4, 6, 6, 4, 4) rows—18 (19, 21, 23, 24, 26) sts rem each side. Work even until armhole measures 2¾ (3¼, 3½, 4, 4½, 4¾)″ (7 [8, 9, 10, 11.5, 12] cm), ending with a WS row.

Shape neck

Next row: (RS) Knit to last 2 (2, 2, 3, 3, 3) sts of left front, place last 2 (2, 2, 3, 3, 3) sts onto holder; on other side, k2 (2, 2, 3, 3, 3) sts and place onto holder, knit to end of row—16 (17, 19, 20, 21, 23) sts rem each side.

BO every other row at neck edge 2 sts once, then 1 st once—13 (14, 16, 17, 18, 20) sts rem each side.

Work even until armhole measures 7 (7½, 7¾, 8¼, 8¾, 9)″ (18 [19, 20, 21, 22, 23] cm), ending with a WS row.

Shape shoulders

BO 7 (7, 8, 9, 9, 10) sts at beg of next 2 rows, then 6 (7, 8, 8, 9, 10) sts at beg of next 2 rows.

Pocket linings (make 2)

With larger needles and RS of front facing, pick up and k21 sts in pocket cast-on sts.

Row 1: (WS) CO 1 st (edge st), purl to end, CO 1 st (edge st).

Row 2: Knit.

Row 3: K1 (edge st), purl to last st, k1 (edge st).

Rep Rows 2 and 3 until lining measures 6″ (15 cm), ending with a RS row. BO all sts.

Sew pocket linings to WS.

SLEEVES

With larger needles, CO 45 (45, 49, 49, 53, 53) sts.

Row 1: (WS) K1 (edge st), k3, *p1, k3; rep from * to last st, k1 (edge st).

Row 2: K1 (edge st), p3, *k1, p3; rep from * to last st, k1 (edge st).

Rep Rows 1 and 2 until sleeve measures 6″ (15 cm) from beg, ending with a WS row.

Next (dec) row: (RS) K7 (7, 3, 3, 5, 5), *k2tog, k8 (8, 6, 6, 6, 6); rep from * 2 (2, 4, 4, 4, 4) more times, k2tog, k6 (6, 4, 4, 6, 6)—41 (41, 43, 43, 47, 47) sts rem.

Next row: K1 (edge st), purl to last st, k1 (edge st).

Next (inc) row: (RS) K1 (edge st), M1, knit to last st, M1, k1 (edge st).

Continue in St st and rep inc row every 6 rows 0 (0, 0, 4, 4, 5) times, every 8 rows 0 (7, 7, 4, 4, 4) times, then every 6 rows 0 (0, 0, 4, 4, 5) times—51 (55, 57, 59, 63, 65) sts. Work even until sleeve measures 17¾ (18, 18½, 19, 19¼, 19¾)″ (45 [46, 47, 48, 49, 50] cm) from beg, ending with a WS row.

SHAPE CAP

BO 5 (5, 6, 7, 8, 9) sts at beg of next 2 rows, then 1 st at beg of next 2 rows—39 (43, 43, 43, 45, 45) sts rem.

Work 2 (0, 2, 2, 2, 2) rows even.

Next (dec) row: (RS) K1 (edge st), k2tog, knit to last 3 sts, ssk, k1 (edge st)—2 sts dec'd.

Rep dec row every 4 rows 0 (0, 0, 1, 2, 3) more time(s), then every other row 7 (9, 9, 8, 7, 6) times—23 (23, 23, 23, 25, 25) sts. Work 1 row even.

Next (double dec) row: (RS) K1 (edge st), k3tog, knit to last 4 sts, sssk, k1 (edge st)—4 sts dec'd.

Rep double dec row once more—15 (15, 15, 15, 17, 17) sts rem.

BO rem sts.

FINISHING

Weave in ends. Block pieces to finished measurements.

Sew shoulder seams.

Collar

With smaller needles and WS facing, beg at left front, k 2 (2, 2, 3, 3, 3) sts from holder, pick up and k18 sts along left neck edge, k21 (21, 21, 23, 23, 23) sts from back holder, pick up and k18 (18, 18, 17, 17, 17) along right neck edge, k2 (2, 2, 3, 3, 3) sts from holder—61 (61, 61, 64, 64, 64) sts.

Row 1: (WS of collar) K1 (edge st), k2, *p1, k2; rep from * to last st, k1 (edge st).

Row 2: K1 (edge st), p2, *k1, p2; rep from * to last st, k1 (edge st).

Rep Rows 1 and 2 twice more.

Next (inc) row: K1 (edge st), k1, M1, k1, *p1, k1, M1, k1; rep from * to last st, k1 (edge st)—81 (81, 81, 85, 85, 85) sts.

Next row: K1 (edge st), p3, *k1, p3; rep from * to last st, k1 (edge st).

Next row: K1 (edge st), k3, *p1, k3; rep from * to last st, k1 (edge st).

Rep last 2 rows until collar measures 6″ (15 cm), ending with a collar WS row. BO all sts loosely knitwise.

Right placket

With smaller needles and RS facing, beg at bottom of split, pick up and knit 4 sts for every 5 rows along edge to neck bind-off, pick up and purl 4 sts for every 5 rows along edge of collar.

Row 1: *K1, p1; rep from * to end, CO 1 st for edge st.

Row 2: K1 (edge st), work in rib as est to end.

Row 3: Work in rib to last st, k1 (edge st).

Rep Rows 2 and 3 until placket measures about 2″ (5 cm). BO loosely in rib.

Left placket

With smaller needles and RS facing, beg at top edge of collar, pick up and purl 4 sts for every 5 rows along edge to neck bind-off, pick up and knit 4 sts for every 5 rows along edge to bottom of split.

Row 1: CO 1 for edge st, *k1, p1; rep from * to end.

Row 2: Work in rib as est to last st, k1 (edge st).

Row 3: K1 (edge st), work in rib to end.

Rep Rows 2 and 3 until placket measures about 2″ (5 cm). BO loosely in rib.

Sew ends plackets bound-off edge of split.

With crochet hook, join yarn to right placket about 4″ (10 cm) from bottom of split, ch 15. Fasten off. Sew end of chain to placket to form button loop.

Sew button to left placket opposite loop.

Sew side and sleeve seams. Sew in sleeves.

Lacy Sweater with Ruffled Edges

This vintage 1950s-style sweater has a ruffled collar and lower edge. It goes well with the gloves in the next pattern.

Photo page 36

finished measurements

31 (33¾, 36½, 39¼, 42¾, 47)" (78.5 [85.5, 92.5, 99.5, 108.5, 119.5] cm) bust circumference and 20¾ (21¾, 22½, 23¼, 24, 24¾)" (53 [55, 57, 59, 61, 63] cm) long. To fit woman's sizes x-small (small, medium, large, 1X, 2X). Shown in size medium.

yarn

Baby weight (fine #2).

Marks & Kattens Eco Baby Wool (100% eco-wool; 91 yd [83 m]/25 g): beige 174, 13 (14, 15, 17, 18, 20) balls.

needles

U.S. size 6 (4 mm): straight and 32" (80 cm) long circular (cir) needles.

Adjust needle sizes if necessary to obtain the correct gauge.

notions

Stitch holders; tapestry needle; three ⅞" (22 mm) buttons.

gauge

23 sts and 34 rows = 4" (10 cm) in patt.

Row 10: K1 (edge st), p4, *sssk, k1, k3tog, p4; rep from * to last st, k1 (edge st)—139 (153, 160, 174, 188, 202) sts.

Row 11: K1 (edge st), k4, *p3, k4; rep from * to last st, k1 (edge st).

Row 12: K1 (edge st), p4, *sk2p, p4; rep from * to last st, k1 (edge st)—101 (111, 116, 126, 136, 146) sts.

Row 13: K1 (edge st, k4, *p1, k4); rep from * to last st, k1 (edge st).

Row 14: Knit.

Row 15: K1 (edge st), purl to last st and dec 2 (3, 2, 3, 1, 2) st(s) evenly spaced, k1 (edge st)—99 (108, 114, 123, 135, 144) sts.

Row 16: K1 (edge st), k1, *(yo) twice, sk2p; rep from * to last 2 sts, k1, k1 (edge st).

Row 17: K1 (edge st), p1, *(k1, p1) in double yo, p1; rep from * to last st, k1 (edge st).

Next (inc) row: (RS) Knit and inc 2 (1, 2, 2, 0, 3) st(s) evenly spaced—101 (109, 117, 125, 135, 147) sts.

Next row: K1 (edge st), purl to last st, k1 (edge st).

Next row: Knit.

Rep last 2 rows twice more, then rep WS row once more.

Change to Lace Patt and work as foll:

Row 1: (RS) K1 (edge st), beg at your size at right side of Lace Patt back chart and work 2 (6, 4, 2, 7, 7) sts, rep next 6 sts 16 (16, 18, 20, 20, 22) times, work rem 1 (5, 3, 1, 6, 6) st(s) of chart, k1 (edge st).

Row 2: K1 (edge st), beg at your size at left side of chart and work 1 (5, 3, 1, 6, 6) st(s), rep next 6 sts 16 (16, 18, 20, 20, 22) times, work rem 2 (6, 4, 2, 7, 7) sts, k1 (edge st).

Next (dec) row: (RS) K1 (edge st), ssk, work in est patt to last 3 sts, k2tog, k1 (edge st)—2 sts dec'd.

Rep dec row every 20 rows 4 more times—91 (99, 107, 115, 125, 137) sts rem. Work even until piece measures 13½ (13¾, 14¼, 14½, 15, 15¼)" (34 [35, 36, 37, 38, 39] cm) from beg, ending with a WS row.

Notes

Circular needles can be used for the back and collar to accommodate the large number of stitches. Do not join. When the back ruffle is completed, change to straight needles if desired.

If a chart row begins or ends with a (yarnover, k2tog), knit those stitches.

To maintain stitch counts while shaping, if a yarnover cannot be worked with its accompanying k2tog or vice versa, work that stitch in stockinette.

BACK

With straight or cir needles, CO 215 (237, 248, 270, 292, 314) sts.

Row 1: (WS) Knit.

Row 2: (RS) K1 (edge st), p4, *k7, p4; rep from * to last st, k1 (edge st).

Row 3: (WS) K1 (edge st), k4, *p7, k4; rep from * to last st, k1 (edge st).

Rows 4–9: Rep Rows 2 and 3 three more times.

Shape armholes

BO 8 (9, 11, 11, 13, 16) sts at beg of next 2 rows, 4 sts at beg of next 0 (0, 0, 0, 0, 2) rows, 3 sts at beg of next 0 (0, 0, 2, 2, 0) rows, 2 sts at beg of next 2 rows, then 1 st at beg of next 6 (6, 6, 4, 6, 6) rows—65 (71, 75, 79, 83, 87) sts. Work even until armhole measures 6¾ (7, 7½, 7¾, 8¼, 8¾)" (17 [18, 19, 20, 21, 22] cm), ending with a WS row.

Shape shoulders and neck

Next row: (RS) BO 7 (8, 8, 9, 9, 10) sts, work 14 (16, 17, 18, 19, 20) sts, place center 23 (23, 25, 25, 27, 27) sts onto holder for neck, join a second ball of yarn and work to end.

Next row: BO 7 (8, 8, 9, 9, 10) sts, purl to last 2 sts of left shoulder, p2tog; on other side, BO 1 st, purl to end.

Next row: BO 6 (7, 8, 8, 9, 9) sts, work to last 2 sts of right shoulder, k2tog; on other side, BO 1 st, work to end.

Next row: BO 6 (7, 8, 8, 9, 9) sts, purl to neck; on other side, purl to end.

BO 6 (7, 7, 8, 8, 9) sts at beg of next 2 rows.

LEFT FRONT

With straight needles, CO 109 (120, 131, 131, 142, 153) sts.

Row 1: (WS) Knit.

Row 2: (RS) K1 (edge st), p4, *k7, p4; rep from * to last 5 sts, k5 (front band).

Row 3: K5 (front band), p4, *k7, p4; rep from * to last st, k1 (edge st).

Rows 4–9: Rep Rows 2 and 3 three more times.

Row 10: K1 (edge st), p4, *sssk, k1, k3tog, p4; rep from * to last 5 sts, k5—73 (80, 87, 87, 94, 101) sts.

Row 11: K5, *k4, p3; rep from * to last 5 sts, k4, k1 (edge st).

Row 12: K1 (edge st), p4, *sk2p, p4; rep from * to last 5 sts, k5—55 (60, 65, 65, 70, 75) sts.

Row 13: K5, *k4, p1; rep from * to last 5 sts, k4, k1 (edge st).

Row 14: Knit.

Row 15: K5, purl to last st and dec 0 (2, 4, 1, 0, 2) st(s) evenly spaced, k1 (edge st)—55 (58, 61, 64, 70, 73) sts.

Row 16: K1 (edge st), k1, *(yo) twice, sk2p; rep from * to last 5 sts, k5.

Row 17: K5, p1, *(k1 p1) in double yo, p1; rep from * to last st, k1 (edge st).

Size 31 (33¾)" only

Next (dec) row: (RS) Knit and dec 2 (1) st(s) evenly spaced—53 (57) sts.

Sizes 36½ (42¾)" only

Next row: (RS) Knit—61 (70) sts.

Sizes 39¼ (47)" only

Next (inc) row: (RS) Knit and inc 1 (3) st(s) evenly spaced—65 (76) sts.

All sizes

Next row: (WS) K5, purl to last st, k1 (edge st).

Next row: Knit.

Rep last 2 rows twice more, then rep WS row once more.

Change to Lace Patt and work as foll:

Row 1: (RS) K1 (edge st), beg at your size at right side of Lace Patt front chart and work 2 (6, 4, 2, 7, 7) sts, rep next 6 sts 7 (7, 8, 9, 9, 10) times, work rem 3 sts of chart, k5 (front band).

Row 2: K5 (front band), beg at left side of chart and work 3 sts, rep next 6 sts 7 (7, 8, 9, 9, 10) times, work rem 2 (6, 4, 2, 7, 7) sts, k1 (edge st).

Next (dec) row: (RS) K1 (edge st), ssk, work in est patt to end— 1 st dec'd.

Rep dec row every 20 rows 4 more times—48 (52, 56, 60, 65, 71) sts rem. Work even until piece measures 13½ (13¾, 14¼, 14½, 15, 15¼)" (34 [35, 36, 37, 38, 39] cm) from beg, ending with a WS row.

Shape armhole and neck

Next row: (RS) BO 8 (9, 11, 11, 13, 16) sts, work to last 8 sts, k2tog, k6—39 (42, 44, 48, 51, 54) sts.

Continue BO at beg of RS rows 4 sts 0 (0, 0, 0, 0, 1) time, 3 sts 0 (0, 0, 1, 1, 0) time, 2 sts once, then 1 st 3 (3, 3, 2, 3, 3) times and, AT THE SAME TIME, dec at end of every RS row 10 (10, 10, 8, 8, 6) more times, then every 4 rows 5 (5, 6, 8, 9, 11) times—19 (22, 23, 25, 26, 28) sts rem when shaping is complete.

Work even until armhole measures 6¾ (7, 7½, 7¾, 8¼, 8¾)" (17 [18, 19, 20, 21, 22] cm), ending with a WS row.

Shape shoulder

BO at beg of RS rows 10 sts 0 (0, 0, 0, 0, 1) time, 9 sts 0 (0, 1, 2, 2) time(s), 8 sts 0 (1, 2, 2, 1, 0) time(s), 7 sts 1 (2, 1, 0, 0, 0) times, then 6 sts 2 (0, 0, 0, 0, 0) times.

RIGHT FRONT

With straight needles, CO 109 (120, 131, 131, 142, 153) sts.

Row 1: (WS) Knit.

Row 2: (RS) K5 (front band), p4, *k7, p4; rep from * to last st, k1 (edge st).

Row 3: K1 (edge st), p4, *k7, p4; rep from * to last 5 sts, k5 (front band).

Rows 4–9: Rep Rows 2 and 3 three more times.

Row 10: K5, p4, *sssk, k1, k3tog, p4; rep from * to last st, k1 (edge st)—73 (80, 87, 87, 94, 101) sts.

Row 11: K1 (edge st), *k4, p3; rep from * to last 9 sts, k4, k5 (front band).

Row 12: K5, p4, *sk2p, p4; rep from * to last st, k1 (edge st)—55 (60, 65, 65, 70, 75) sts.

Row 13: K1 (edge st), *k4, p1; rep from * to last 9 sts, k4, k5 (front band).

Row 14: Knit.

Row 15: K1 (edge st), purl to last 5 sts and dec 0 (2, 4, 1, 0, 2) st(s) evenly spaced, k5—55 (58, 61, 64, 70, 73) sts.

Row 16: K5 (front band), k1, *(yo) twice, sk2p; rep from * to last st, k1 (edge st).

Row 17: K1 (edge st), p1, *(k1 p1) in double yo, p1; rep from * to last 5 sts, k5.

Size 31 (33¾)" only

Next (dec) row: (RS) Knit and dec 2 (1) st(s) evenly spaced—53 (57) sts.

Sizes 36½ (42¾)" only

Next row: (RS) Knit—61 (70) sts.

Sizes 39¼ (47)" only

Next (inc) row: (RS) Knit and inc 1 (3) st(s) evenly spaced—65 (76) sts.

All sizes

Next row: (WS) K1 (edge st), purl to last 5 sts, k5.

Next row: Knit.

Rep last 2 rows twice more, then rep WS row once more.

Change to Lace Patt and work as foll:

Row 1: (RS) K5 (front band), beg at right side of Lace Patt front chart and work 3 sts, rep next 6 sts 7 (7, 8, 9, 9, 10) times, work rem 2 (6, 4, 2, 7, 7) sts of chart, k1 (edge st).

Row 2: K1 (edge st), beg at your size at left side of chart and work 2 (6, 4, 2, 7, 7) sts, rep next 6 sts 7 (7, 8, 9, 9, 10) times, work rem 3 sts, k5 (front band).

Next (dec) row: (RS) K5, work in est patt to last 3 sts, k2tog, k1 (edge st)—1 st dec'd.

Rep dec row every 20 rows 4 more times—48 (52, 56, 60, 65, 71) sts rem.

AT THE SAME TIME, when piece measures 7½ (7½, 7¾, 7¾, 8¼, 8¼)" (19 [19, 20, 20, 21, 21] cm) from beg, work buttonhole on next RS row as foll:

Buttonhole row: K2, BO 2, k1, work in est patt to end.

Lace Pattern, back

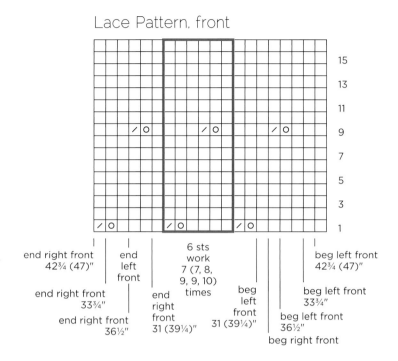

end
42¾ (47)"

end
36½"

end
33¾"

end
31 (39¼)"

6 sts
work
16 (16, 18,
20, 20, 22)
times

beg
36½"

beg
42¾ (47)"

beg
31 (39¼)"

beg
33¾"

Lace Pattern, front

end right front
42¾ (47)"

end right front
33¾"

end right front
36½"

end
left
front

end
right
front

end
right
front
31 (39¼)"

6 sts
work
7 (7, 8,
9, 9, 10)
times

beg
left
front

beg
left
front
31 (39¼)"

beg left front
42¾ (47)"

beg left front
33¾"

beg left front
36½"

beg right front

Lace Pattern, sleeve

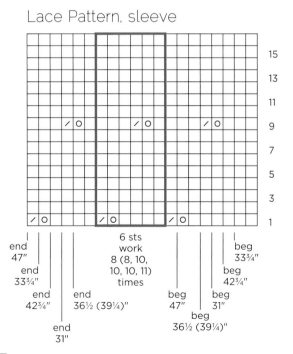

end
47"

end
33¾"

end
42¾"

end
31"

end
36½ (39¼)"

6 sts
work
8 (8, 10,
10, 10, 11)
times

beg
47"

beg
36½ (39¼)"

beg
31"

beg
33¾"

beg
42¾"

☐ k on RS; p on WS

• p on RS; k on WS

Ⓞ yo

⟋ k2tog

☐ pattern repeat

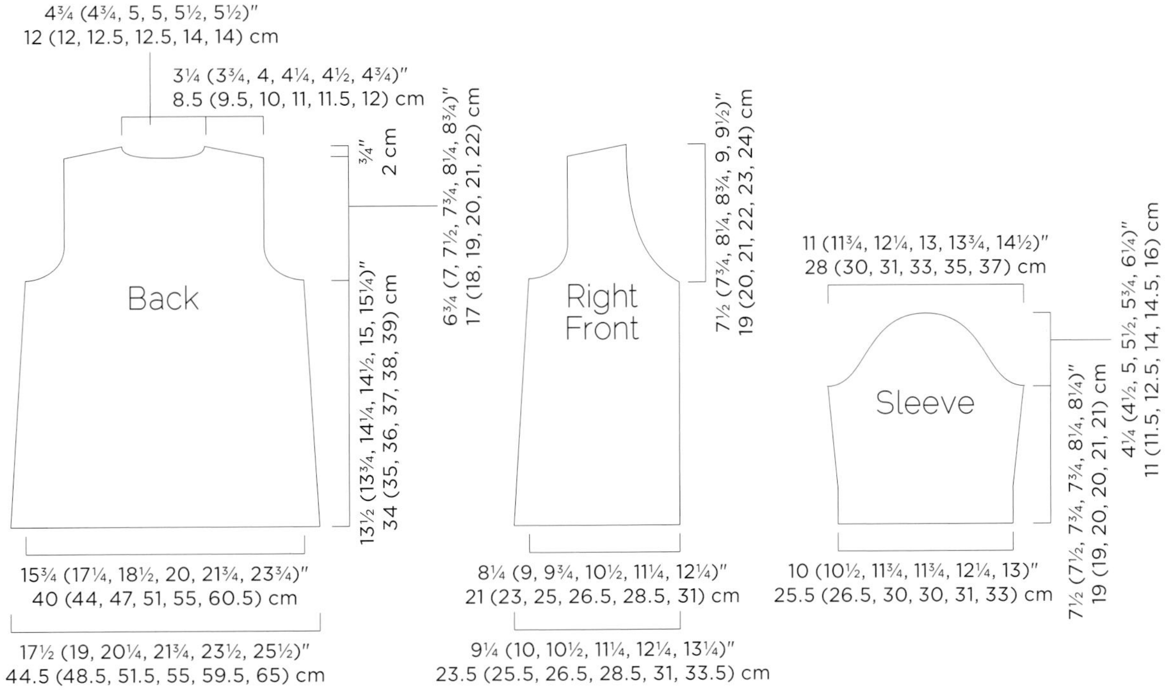
4¾ (4¾, 5, 5, 5½, 5½)"
12 (12, 12.5, 12.5, 14, 14) cm
3¼ (3¾, 4, 4¼, 4½, 4¾)"
8.5 (9.5, 10, 11, 11.5, 12) cm
¾"
2 cm
6¾ (7, 7½, 7¾, 8¼, 8¾)"
17 (18, 19, 20, 21, 22) cm
13½ (13¾, 14¼, 14½, 15, 15¼)"
34 (35, 36, 37, 38, 39) cm
Back
15¾ (17¼, 18½, 20, 21¾, 23¾)"
40 (44, 47, 51, 55, 60.5) cm
17½ (19, 20¼, 21¾, 23½, 25½)"
44.5 (48.5, 51.5, 55, 59.5, 65) cm
Right
Front
7½ (7¾, 8¼, 8¾, 9, 9½)"
19 (20, 21, 22, 23, 24) cm
8¼ (9, 9¾, 10½, 11¼, 12¼)"
21 (23, 25, 26.5, 28.5, 31) cm
9¼ (10, 10½, 11¼, 12¼, 13¼)"
23.5 (25.5, 26.5, 28.5, 31, 33.5) cm
11 (11¾, 12¼, 13, 13¾, 14½)"
28 (30, 31, 33, 35, 37) cm
Sleeve
4¼ (4½, 5, 5½, 5¾, 6¼)"
11 (11.5, 12.5, 14, 14.5, 16) cm
7½ (7½, 7¾, 7¾, 8¼, 8¼)"
19 (19, 20, 20, 21, 21) cm
10 (10½, 11¾, 11¾, 12¼, 13)"
25.5 (26.5, 30, 30, 31, 33) cm

Next row: CO 2 sts over buttonhole gap. Rep buttonhole row with 22 (22, 24, 24, 24, 26) rows between; last buttonhole should be about ⅜" (1 cm) below beg of neck shaping.

Work even until piece measures 13½ (13¾, 14¼, 14½, 15, 15¼)" (34 [35, 36, 37, 38, 39] cm) from beg, ending with a RS row.

Shape armhole and neck

Next row: (WS) BO 8 (9, 11, 11, 13, 16) sts, work to end—40 (43, 45, 49, 52, 55) sts.

Next (neck dec) row: (RS) K6, ssk, work in established patt to end—1 st dec'd.

Continue BO at beg of WS rows 4 sts 0 (0, 0, 0, 0, 1) time, 3 sts 0 (0, 0, 1, 1, 0) time, 2 sts once, then 1 st 3 (3, 3, 2, 3, 3) times and, AT THE SAME TIME, dec at beg of every RS row 10 (10, 10, 8, 8, 6) more times, then every 4 rows 5 (5, 6, 8, 9, 11) times—19 (22, 23, 25, 26, 28) sts rem when shaping is complete.

Work even until armhole measures 6¾ (7, 7½, 7¾, 8¼, 8¾)" (17 [18, 19, 20, 21, 22] cm), ending with a RS row.

Shape shoulder

BO at beg of WS rows 10 sts 0 (0, 0, 0, 0, 1) time, 9 sts 0 (0, 0, 1, 2, 2) time(s), 8 sts 0 (1, 2, 2, 1, 0) time(s), 7 sts 1 (2, 1, 0, 0, 0) time(s), then 6 sts 2 (0, 0, 0, 0, 0) times.

SLEEVES

With straight needles, CO 123 (134, 145, 145, 156, 167) sts.

Row 1: (WS) Knit.

Row 2: (RS) K1 (edge st), *k7, p4; rep from * to last st, k1 (edge st).

Row 3: (WS) K1 (edge st), *k4, p7; rep from * to last st, k1 (edge st).

Rows 4–9: Rep Rows 2 and 3 three more times.

Row 10: K1 (edge st), *sssk, k1, k3tog, p4; rep from * to last st, k1 (edge st)—79 (86, 93, 93, 100, 107) sts.

Row 11: K1 (edge st), *k4, p3; rep from * to last st, k1 (edge st).

Row 12: K1 (edge st), *sk2p, p4; rep from * to last st, k1 (edge st)—57 (62, 67, 67, 72, 77) sts.

Row 13: K1 (edge st), *k4, p1; rep from * to last st, k1 (edge st).

Row 14: Knit.

Row 15: K1 (edge st), purl to last st and dec 3 (2, 1, 1, 3, 2) st(s) across, k1 (edge st)—54 (60, 66, 66, 69, 75) sts.

Row 16: K1 (edge st), k1, *(yo) twice, sk2p; rep from * to last st, k1 (edge st).

Row 17: K1 (edge st), p1, *(k1, p1) in double yo, p1; rep from * to last st, k1 (edge st).

Next (inc) row: (RS) Knit and inc 3 (1, 1, 1, 2, 0) st(s) evenly spaced—57 (61, 67, 67, 71, 75) sts.

Next row: (WS) K1 (edge st), purl to last st, k1 (edge st).

Next row: Knit.

Rep last 2 rows twice more, then rep WS row once more.

Change to Lace Patt and work as foll:

Row 1: (RS) K1 (edge st), beg at your size at right side of Lace Patt sleeve chart and work 4 (6, 3, 3, 5, 1) st(s), rep next 6 sts 8 (8, 10, 10, 10, 11) times, work rem 3 (5, 2, 2, 4, 6) sts of chart, k1 (edge st).

Row 2: K1 (edge st), beg at your size at left side of Lace Patt sleeve chart and work 3 (5, 2, 2, 4, 6) sts, rep next 6 sts 8 (8, 10, 10, 10, 11) times, work rem 4 (6, 3, 3, 5, 1) st(s), k1 (edge st).

Next (inc) row: (RS) K1 (edge st), M1, work in est patt to last st, M1, k1 (edge st)—2 sts inc'd.

Rep inc row every 12 (12, 18, 10, 10, 10) rows 2 (2, 1, 3, 3, 3) more time(s)—63 (67, 71, 75, 79, 83) sts.

Work even until piece measures 7½ (7½, 7¾, 7¾, 8¼, 8¼)" (19 [19, 20, 20, 21, 21] cm) from beg, ending with a WS row.

Shape cap

BO 6 (7, 8, 9, 10, 12) sts at beg of next 2 rows, then 1 st at beg of next 2 rows—49 (51, 53, 55, 57) sts. Work 2 rows even.

Next (dec) row: (RS) K1 (edge st), k2tog, work in est patt to last 3 sts, ssk, k1 (edge st)—2 sts dec'd.

Rep dec row every 4 rows 2 (2, 4, 5, 6, 8) more times and then every RS row 9 (10, 8, 8, 7, 5) times—25 (25, 27, 27, 29, 29) sts.

Work 1 row even.

Next (double dec) row: (RS) K1 (edge st), k3tog, work to last 4 sts, sssk, k1 (edge st)—4 sts dec'd.

Rep double dec row once more—17 (17, 19, 19, 21, 21) sts.

BO rem sts.

FINISHING

Weave in ends. Block pieces to finished measurements.

Sew shoulder seams.

Collar

With cir needle and WS facing, pick up and k49 (49, 52, 52, 55, 55) sts along shaped edge of left neck, k23 (23, 25, 25, 27, 27) sts from back neck holder, pick up and k49 (49, 52, 52, 55, 55) sts along shaped edge of right neck—121 (121, 129, 129, 137, 137) sts.

Row 1: (WS of collar) K5 (edge sts), purl to last 5 sts, k5 (edge sts).

Row 2: Knit.

Rows 3–5: Rep Rows 1 and 2 once more, then rep Row 1 once.

Row 6: K5 (edge sts), purl to last 5 sts and inc 13 (13, 14, 14, 15, 15) sts evenly spaced, k5 (edge sts)—134 (134, 143, 143, 152, 152) sts.

Row 7: Rep Row 1.

Row 8: K5 (edge sts), k1, *(yo) twice, sk2p; rep from * to last 5 sts, k5 (edge sts).

Row 9: K5 (edge sts), p1, *(k1, p1) in double yo, p1; rep from * to last 5 sts, k5 (edge sts).

Row 10: K5 (edge sts), knit to last 5 sts and inc 0 (0, 1, 1, 2, 2) st(s) evenly spaced, k5 (edge sts)—134 (134, 144, 144, 154, 154) sts.

Row 11: K5 (edge sts), purl to last 5 sts, k5 (edge sts).

Row 12: K5 (edge sts), p4, *k1, p4; rep from * to last 5 sts, k5 (edge sts).

Row 13: K5 (edge sts), k4, *p1, k4; rep from * to last 5 sts, k5 (edge sts).

Row 14: K5 (edge sts), p4, *yo, k1, yo, p4; rep from * to last 5 sts, k5 (edge sts)—182 (182, 196, 196, 210, 210) sts.

Row 15: K5 (edge sts), k4, *p3, k4; rep from * to last 5 sts, k5 (edge sts).

Row 16: K5 (edge sts), p4, *yo, k3, yo, p4; rep from * to last 5 sts, k5 (edge sts)—230 (230, 248, 248, 266, 266) sts.

Row 17: K5 (edge sts), k4, *p5, k4; rep from * to last 5 sts, k5 (edge sts).

Row 18: K5 (edge sts), p4, *yo, k5, yo, p4; rep from * to last 5 sts, k5 (edge sts)—278, 278, 300, 300, 322, 322) sts.

Row 19: K5 (edge sts), k4, *p7, k4; rep from * to last 5 sts, k5 (edge sts).

Row 20: K5 (edge sts), p4, *k7, p4; rep from * to last 5 sts, k5 (edge sts).

Rows 21–25: Rep Rows 20 and 21 two more times, then rep Row 20 once more with 2 more sts between yo's every even-number row and 2 more knit sts in each rep on every odd-numbered row.

Row 26: Knit.

BO loosely knitwise.

Sew side and sleeve seams. Sew in sleeves. Sew buttons to left front band opposite buttonholes.

20 (20) sts. Pm for beg of rnd. Work in St st until thumb measures 2 (2¼)" (5 [5.5] cm).

Next (dec) rnd: *K2tog; rep from * end—10 (10) sts.

Knit 1 rnd even.

Rep dec rnd once more—5 sts. Cut yarn, draw tail through rem sts, and pull tight to secure.

LEFT GLOVE

Work left glove as for right until piece measures 2¼ (2½)" (5.5 [6.5] cm) from dec rnd.

Next rnd: Knit to last 9 sts, k9 with a piece of contrasting waste yarn, sl sts just knit back to left needle and knit again with main yarn.

Continue same as for right glove.

Short-Sleeve Vest

This vest, with a narrow collar and cap sleeves, is closed with a belt or shawl pin. You can vary the look by adding a fringe edging around the collar and experimenting with different closures.

Photos page 37

finished measurements

32½ (35¾, 39, 43¼, 46½, 50¾)" (82.5 [91, 99, 110, 118, 129] cm) bust circumference and 30 (30¾, 31½, 32¼, 33, 34)" (76 [78, 80, 82, 84, 86] cm) long. To fit woman's sizes x-small (small, medium, large, 1X, 2X). Shown in size medium.

yarn

Worsted weight (medium #4).

Marks & Kattens Eco Wool (100% eco-wool; 88 yd [80 m]/50 g): beige 1980, 9 (10, 11, 12, 13, 14) balls.

needles

U.S. size 10½ (6.5 mm) needles.

Adjust needle size if necessary to obtain the correct gauge.

notions

U.S. size J-10 (6 mm) crochet hook; stitch holders; tapestry needle; shawl pin or belt.

gauge

15 sts and 21 rows = 4" (10 cm) in St st.

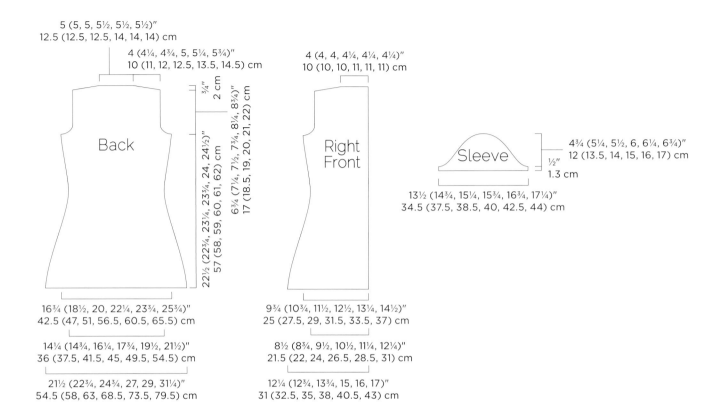

5 (5, 5, 5½, 5½, 5½)"
12.5 (12.5, 12.5, 14, 14, 14) cm

4 (4¼, 4¾, 5, 5¼, 5¾)"
10 (11, 12, 12.5, 13.5, 14.5) cm

4 (4, 4, 4¼, 4¼, 4¼)"
10 (10, 10, 11, 11, 11) cm

Back

Right Front

Sleeve

¾"
2 cm

6¾ (7¼, 7½, 7¾, 8¼, 8¾)"
17 (18.5, 19, 20, 21, 22) cm

22½ (22¾, 23¼, 23¾, 24, 24½)"
57 (58, 59, 60, 61, 62) cm

4¾ (5¼, 5½, 6, 6¼, 6¾)"
12 (13.5, 14, 15, 16, 17) cm

½"
1.3 cm

13½ (14¾, 15¼, 15¾, 16¾, 17¼)"
34.5 (37.5, 38.5, 40, 42.5, 44) cm

16¾ (18½, 20, 22¼, 23¾, 25¾)"
42.5 (47, 51, 56.5, 60.5, 65.5) cm

14¼ (14¾, 16¼, 17¾, 19½, 21½)"
36 (37.5, 41.5, 45, 49.5, 54.5) cm

21½ (22¾, 24¾, 27, 29, 31¼)"
54.5 (58, 63, 68.5, 73.5, 79.5) cm

9¾ (10¾, 11½, 12½, 13¼, 14½)"
25 (27.5, 29, 31.5, 33.5, 37) cm

8½ (8¾, 9½, 10½, 11¼, 12¼)"
21.5 (22, 24, 26.5, 28.5, 31) cm

12¼ (12¾, 13¾, 15, 16, 17)"
31 (32.5, 35, 38, 40.5, 43) cm

FINISHING

Weave in ends. Block pieces to finished measurements.

Sew shoulder seams.

Collar

Place sts from all holders onto needle—49 (49, 49, 53, 53, 53) sts. Join yarn to beg with a WS row.

Row 1: (WS) K2 (edge sts), purl to last 2 sts, k2 (edge sts).

Row 2: Knit.

Rep Rows 1 and 2 until collar measures 2½" (6 cm), ending with a WS row.

Next (dec) row: (RS) K2 (edge sts), k2tog, knit to last 4 sts, ssk, k2 (edge sts)—2 sts dec'd.

Rep dec row every RS row 3 more times—41 (41, 41, 45, 45, 45) sts.

Work 3 rows even. BO rem sts.

Sew side and sleeve seams. Sew in sleeves.

With crochet hook and RS facing, beg on lower edge at right side seam, work 1 rnd of sc, working 1 sc in each st along lower edge, 1 sc in every other row along front edges and collar, and 1 sc in each st along bound-off row of collar.

Optional: With crochet hook, create fringe (see page 159) in each sc along front edges.

Pleated Cap, Gloves, Leg Warmers, and Neck Warmer

These accessories will keep you cozy and warm when the cold comes. Worked in simple knit and purl, they also have a fun pleat structure.

Photo page 38

finished measurements

CAP // 22" (56 cm) brim circumference and 11" (28 cm) long with edge rolled.

GLOVES // 9" (23 cm) hand circumference and 12¼" (31 cm) long with edge rolled.

LEG WARMERS // 14½" (37 cm) top circumference and 16½" (42 cm) long with edges rolled.

NECK WARMER // 32" (81.5 cm) circumference and 12½" (31.5 cm) long with edges rolled.

yarn

Worsted weight (medium #4).

Marks & Kattens Eco Wool (100% eco-wool; 88 yd [80 m]/50 g): beige 1980, 3 balls for cap, 3 balls for gloves, 5 balls for leg warmers, 5 balls for neck warmer.

needles

CAP // U.S. size 8 (5 mm): 16" (40 cm) circular (cir) and set of 4 or 5 double-pointed needles (dpn).

GLOVES // U.S. size 9 (5.5 mm): straight and set of 5 double-pointed needles (dpn).

LEG WARMERS // U.S. size 9 (5.5 mm): set of 5 double-pointed needles (dpn).

NECK WARMER // U.S. size 10 (6 mm): 24" (60 cm) circular (cir) needle.

Adjust needle sizes if necessary to obtain the correct gauge.

notions

Stitch markers (m); stitch holders; waste yarn; tapestry needle.

gauge

18 sts and 26 rows = 4" (10 cm) in patt on U.S. size 8 (5 mm) needles.

16½ sts and 23 rows = 4" (10 cm) in St st on U.S. size 9 (5.5 mm) needles.

14½ sts and 30 rows = 4" (10 cm) in patt on U.S. size 10 (6 mm) needles.

Notes

The cap, leg warmers, and neck warmer are worked with the purl side out.

Stitch markers are used to mark the beginning of rounds; slip markers every round.

CAP

With size 8 (5 mm) cir needle, CO 90 sts and join, being careful not to twist sts. Place marker (pm) for beg of rnd.

Rnds 1–12: Purl.

Rnd 13 (tuck): *(Purl the next st tog with the st 6 rows below) 9 times, p6; rep from * 5 more times.

Rnds 14–25: Purl.

Rnd 26 (tuck): *P3, (purl the next st tog with the st 6 rows below) 4 times, p4, (purl the next st tog with the st 6 rows below) 4 times; rep from * 5 more times.

Rnds 27–42: Purl.

Rnd 43 (tuck): *P6, (purl the next st tog with the st 6 rows below) 9 times; rep from * 5 more times. Rep Rnds 1–43 once more.

Rnds 87 and 88: Purl.

Shape cap

Change to size 8 (5 mm) dpns when there are too few sts on needle to work comfortably.

Rnd 1: *P7, p3tog; rep from * 8 more times—72 sts rem.

Rnds 2 and 3: Purl.

Rnd 4: *P5, p3tog; rep from * 8 more times—54 sts rem.

Rnds 5 and 6: Purl.

Rnd 7: *P3, p3tog; rep from * 8 more times—36 sts rem.

Rnd 8: Purl.

Rnd 9: *P1, p3tog; rep from * 8 more times—18 sts rem.

Rnd 10: Purl.

Rnd 11: (P2tog) around—9 sts rem.

Rnd 12: (P2tog) 4 times, p1—5 sts rem.

Cut yarn, draw tail through rem sts, and pull tight to secure.

Weave in ends. Turn cap with the knit side facing out.

GLOVES
Right glove

Note: The cuff is worked back and forth before joining to work the rest in the round.

With size 9 (5.5 mm) needles, CO 47 sts.

Row 1: (WS) Purl.

Rows 2–12: Work in St st (knit RS rows, purl WS rows).

Row 13: (WS; tuck row) K1 (edge st), p3, *(purl the next st tog with the st 6 rows below) 9 times, p6; rep from * once more, (purl the next st tog with the st 6 rows below) 9 times, p3, k1 (edge st).

Rows 14–24: Work in St st.

Row 25: (WS; tuck row) K1 (edge st), p2, *(purl the next st tog with the st 6 rows below) 5 times, p5; rep from * twice more, p3, k1 (edge st).

Rows 26–40: Work in St st.

Row 41: (WS; tuck row) K1 (edge st), *p6, (purl the next st tog with the st 6 rows below) 9 times: rep from * twice more, k1 (edge st).

Row 42: Knit.

Row 43: BO 1, purl to last 2 sts and dec 5 sts evenly spaced across these sts, BO 1—40 sts.

Change size 8 (5 mm) dpns. Distribute sts evenly over 4 dpns, with 10 sts on each needle. Join to work in the rnd. Place marker (pm) for beg of rnd. Work even in St st (knit every rnd) piece measures 2¾″ (7 cm) from where work was joined.

Next rnd: Knit the first 6 sts with a piece of contrasting waste yarn for thumb opening, sl sts just knit back to left needle and knit again with main yarn. Continue even until piece measures 4¾″ (12 cm) from where work was joined.

INDEX FINGER

Knit first 6 sts, CO 1 st, knit last 6 sts, place rem 28 sts onto holders—13 sts. Join to work in the rnd. Pm for beg of rnd. Work in St st until finger measures 3″ (7.5 cm).

Next (dec) rnd: (K2tog) 6 times, k1—7 sts rem.

Cut yarn, draw tail through rem sts, and pull tight to secure.

MIDDLE FINGER

Place first 6 sts and last 6 sts onto dpns, leave rem 16 sts on st holders. Join yarn, pick up and k1 in CO st at base of index finger, k6, CO 1 st, k6—14 sts. Join to work in the rnd. Pm for beg of rnd. Work in St st until finger measures 3¼″ (8.5 cm).

Next (dec) rnd: (K2tog) 7 times—7 sts rem.

Cut yarn, draw tail through rem sts, and pull tight to secure.

RING FINGER

Place first 4 sts and last 4 sts onto dpns, leave rem 8 sts on st holders. Join yarn, pick up and k1 in CO st at base of index finger, k4, CO 1 st, k4—10 sts. Join to work in the rnd. Pm for beg of rnd. Work in St st until finger measures 3″ (7.5 cm).

Next (dec) rnd: (K2tog) 5 times—5 sts rem.

Cut yarn, draw tail through rem sts, and pull tight to secure.

LITTLE FINGER

Place rem 8 sts onto dpns. Join yarn, pick up and k1 in CO st at base of ring finger—9 sts. Join to work in the rnd. Pm for beg of rnd. Work in St st until finger measures 2½″ (6 cm).

Next (dec) rnd: (K2tog) 4 times, k1—5 sts rem.

Cut yarn, draw tail through rem sts, and pull tight to secure.

THUMB

Remove waste yarn from thumb and arrange 12 revealed sts over 3 size 8 (5 mm) dpns and pick up 1 st at each side of opening—14 sts. Join to work in the rnd. Pm for beg of rnd. Work in St st for 2¼″ (5.5 cm).

Next (dec) rnd: (K2tog) 7 times—7 sts rem.

Cut yarn, draw tail through rem sts, and pull tight to secure.

FINISHING

Sew cuff seam.

Weave in ends.

Left glove

Work left glove as for right until piece measures 2¾″ (7 cm) from where work was joined.

Next rnd: Knit to the last 6 sts, knit the last 6 sts with a piece of contrasting waste yarn for thumb opening, sl sts just knit back to left needle and knit again with main yarn.

Continue same as for right glove.

LEG WARMERS (make 2)

With size 9 (5.5 mm) dpns, CO 60 sts. Divide sts evenly over 4 dpns with 15 sts on each needle and join, being careful not to twist sts. Place marker (pm) for beg of rnd.

Rnds 1–12: Purl.

Rnd 13 (tuck): *(Purl the next st tog with the st 6 rows below) 9 times, p6; rep from * 3 more times.

Rnds 14–25: Purl.

Rnd 26 (tuck): *P3, (purl the next st tog with the st 6 rows below) 4 times, p4, (purl the next st tog with the st 6 rows below) 4 times; rep from * 3 more times.

Rnds 27–42: Purl.

Rnd 43 (tuck): *P6, (purl the next st tog with the st 6 rows below) 9 times; rep from * 3 more times.

Continue in reverse St st (purl every rnd) until piece measures 7" (18 cm) from beg with edge unrolled.

Shape calf

Next (dec) rnd: P1, p2tog, purl to last 3 sts, p2tog, p1— 2 sts dec'd.

Rep dec rnd every 4 rnds 7 more times—44 sts.

Continue even until piece measures 17" (43 cm) from beg.

BO loosely.

Weave in ends. Turn leg warmer with knit side facing out.

NECK WARMER

With size 10 (6 mm) cir needle, CO 120 sts and join, being careful not to twist sts. Place marker (pm) for beg of rnd.

Rnds 1–12: Purl.

Rnd 13 (tuck): *(Purl the next st tog with the st 6 rows below) 9 times, p6; rep from * 7 more times.

Rnds 14–25: Purl.

Rnd 26 (tuck): *(Purl the next st tog with the st 6 rows below) 6 times, p6; rep from * 9 more times.

Rnds 27–42: Purl.

Rnd 43 (tuck): *P6, (purl the next st tog with the st 6 rows below) 9 times; rep from * 7 more times.

Rep Rnds 1–43 once more.

Rnds 87–96: Purl.

BO loosely.

Weave in ends. Turn neck warmer with knit side facing out.

Garter Stitch Shawl

If you are a beginner knitter, this garter stitch shawl is the perfect first project for you. It is worked only with knit stitches in one straight piece and then held together with a shawl pin. It couldn't be easier!

Photo page 39

SHAWL

CO 65 sts. Work in garter st (knit every row) until about 2½ yd (2.3 m) of yarn rem. BO all sts loosely.

finished measurements
About 17¼" (44 cm) wide and 57" (145 cm) long.

yarn
Worsted weight (medium #4).

Marks & Kattens Eco Wool (100% eco-wool; 88 yd [80 m]/50 g): beige 1980, 8 balls.

needles
U.S. size 10¾ (7 mm) needles.

Adjust needle sizes if necessary to obtain the correct gauge.

notions
Shawl pin.

gauge
15 sts and 31 rows = 4" (10 cm) in garter st.

Glossary

Tips for Good Results with Your Knitting

1 // For good results when you knit, it is very important to maintain the correct gauge. If you knit more loosely than the recommended gauge, the garment will be too big, and, if you knit more tightly, the garment will be too small. If the gauge is not correct, try another needle size.

2 // Never change to a new ball of yarn in the middle of a row; always change yarns at the side. Weave in tails neatly on WS.

3 // After all the pieces have been knit, block them to the correct measurements given in the pattern instructions. Lay out a damp towel or piece of fabric over the knit pieces and leave them to dry. This is particularly important when you have knit a textured or cabled garment that draws in.

4 // When finishing, sew the garment with the right sides facing. See the mattress stitch drawing on the next page for seaming instructions.

5 // Always store knitted garments flat; do not hang on a hanger.

Garment Care

1 // Wash with the wrong side out.

2 // Squeeze, but do not wring or twist the garment, because the wool could pill.

3 // Dry the garment flat on a towel and block to finished measurements or it might easily stretch.

4 // Shake the garment when it is half dry to make it fluffier.

5 // Do not wash woolen garments too often. Air them outside instead.

6 // Use environmentally friendly wool wash.

Abbreviations

beg	begin(s), beginning
BO	bind off
cm	centimeter(s)
cn	cable needle
CO	cast on
dec	decrease
dpn	double-pointed needle(s)
est	established
foll	following
inc	increase
k	knit
k1f&b	knit into front and then knit into back of same stitch
k2tog	knit 2 together
k3tog	knit 3 together
m1	make 1 increase
pm	place marker

p	purl
psso	pass slip stitch over
rem	remain(ing)
rep	repeat
rnd(s)	round(s)
RS	right side
ssk	slip 2 stitches knitwise, one at a time, from left needle to right needle, insert left needle tip through both front loops and knit together from this position (1 stitch decreased)
sssk	work as for ssk, slipping 3 sts
st(s)	stitch(es)
St st	stockinette stitch (knit on RS and purl on WS or knit all rounds)
tbl	through back loop(s)
WS	wrong side
yo	yarnover

Techniques

CROCHET

CH (CHAIN STITCH) // Make a loop, *insert hook and pull a loop through; repeat from * until you have the desired number of chain stitches.

SL ST (SLIP STITCH) // Insert hook into top of stitch on previous row, catch yarn and bring through stitch and loop on hook.

SC (SINGLE CROCHET) // Insert hook into top of stitch on previous row, catch yarn and bring a loop through (2 loops now on hook), yarn around hook and pull through the 2 loops on hook.

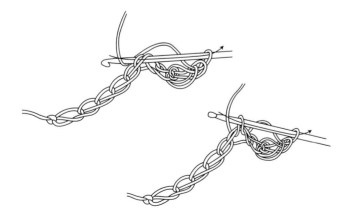

DC (DOUBLE CROCHET) // Yarn around hook and then insert hook into top of stitch on previous row; bring a loop through (3 loops on hook). (Catch yarn and bring through 2 loops) 2 times.

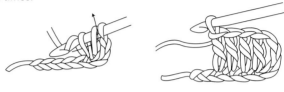

TR (TREBLE CROCHET) // Yarn around hook twice and then insert hook into top of stitch on previous row; bring loop through (4 loops on hook). (Catch yarn and bring through 2 loops) 3 times.

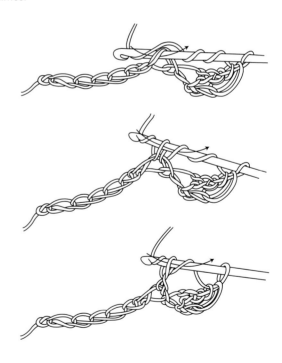

FRINGE

Cut yarn slightly longer than twice the desired fringe length and fold over itself. Insert crochet hook through the loop in the loose yarn and then from WS to RS of the garment. Catch the ends of the yarn and pull through the loop on hook. Trim.

I-CORD

With double-pointed needle, cast on desired number of stitches (usually 3). *Without turning the needle, slide the stitches to the other point, pull yarn around the back, and knit the stitches as usual. Repeat from * for desired length.

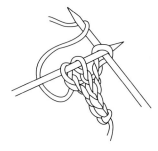

MATTRESS STITCH

Sew inside the edge stitches, with the right side facing you. Insert the needle into one piece vertically and then sew down under the next 2 horizontal strands between the stitches. Insert the needle in the opposite piece vertically and sew down under the next 2 horizontal strands. Always insert needle downward into the same stitch where the yarn came up in the previous stitch.

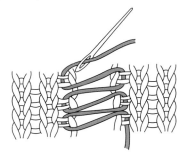

Source for Yarn

MARKS & KATTENS
BOX 274, 431 24 Mölndal
www.marks-kattens.se
www.swedishyarn.com

Indulge your knitting senses

in even more timeless titles from Interweave

French Girl Knits
Innovative Techniques,
Romantic Details, and
Feminine Designs

Kristeen Griffin-Grimes

ISBN 978-1-59668-069-2
$24.95

A Handknit Romance
22 Vintage Designs with
Lovely Details

Jennie Atkinson

ISBN 978-1-59668-779-0
$24.95

Essentially
Feminine Knits
25 Must-Have Chic Designs

Lene Holme Samsøe

ISBN 978-1-59668-784-4
$24.95

---

knitting daily

Knitting Daily is a friendly online community where you'll meet other fiber enthusiasts, learn new techniques and tips from industry experts, meet up-and-coming knitwear designers and celebrity authors, access free knitting patterns, and more!

knitscene

In each issue, we feature up-and-coming designers, popular yarns, fun and concise tutorials, and fresh photography that invites the reader into a yarn-filled daydream. The projects are simple but intriguing, stylish but wearable, and designed for knitters of all ages and sizes.

knitting daily shop
shop.knittingdaily.com